# Grant's Canal

## The Union's Attempt to Bypass Vicksburg

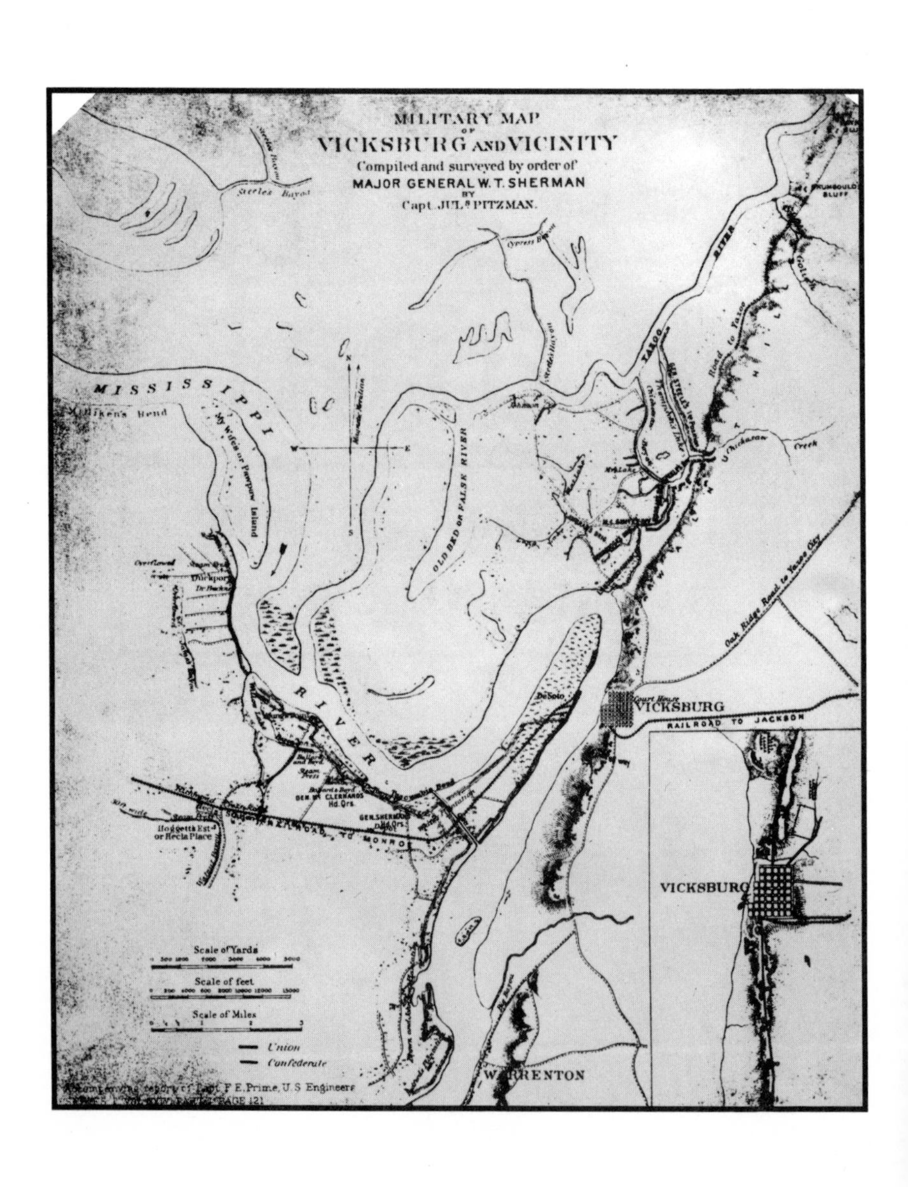
MILITARY MAP OF VICKSBURG AND VICINITY
Compiled and surveyed by order of
MAJOR GENERAL W. T. SHERMAN
BY
Capt. JUL.S PITZMAN.
MISSISSIPPI
RIVER
YAZOO
RIVER
OLD BED OR FALSE RIVER
Milliken's Bend
Cypress Bayou
Steeles Bayou
Chickasaw Creek
Road to Yazoo
Oak Ridge Road to Yazoo City
VICKSBURG
Court House
RAILROAD TO JACKSON
DeSoto
GEN. SHERMAN Hd. Qrs.
Hd. Qrs.
Hodgetts Est. or Hecla Place
WARRENTON
Scale of Yards
Scale of feet
Scale of Miles
Union
Confederate
U. S. Engineers

## The Union's Attempt to Bypass Vicksburg

David F. Bastian

This Burd Street Press book
was printed by
Beidel Printing House, Inc.
63 West Burd Street
Shippensburg, PA 17257 USA

In respect for the scholarship contained herein, the acid-free paper used in this book meets the guidelines for permanence and durability of the Committee on Production Guidelines for Book Longevity of the Council on Library Resources.

For a complete list of available publications
please write
Burd Street Press
Division of White Mane Publishing Co., Inc.
P.O. Box 152
Shippensburg, PA 17257 USA

Library of Congress Cataloging-in-Publication Data

Bastian, David F., 1944–
Grant's canal : the Union's attempt to bypass Vicksburg / David F. Bastian.
p. cm.
Includes index.
ISBN 0–942597–93–1 (alk. paper)
1. Vicksburg (Miss.)– –History– –Civil War, 1861–1865. 2. United States– –History– –Civil War, 1861–1865– –Engineering and construction. 3. Water diversion– –Mississippi River– –History– –19th century.
I. Title.
E474.11.B37 1995
973.7'344– –dc20

95-23875
CIP

PRINTED IN THE UNITED STATES OF AMERICA

# Table Of Contents

# GRANT'S CANAL

A bold attempt to divert the Mississippi River across the base of De Soto Point, Louisiana, was made in 1862 by Brigadier General Thomas Williams of the United States Army. Had he succeeded in that plan to bypass the fortifications at Vicksburg, the single remaining Confederate stronghold on the Mississippi River, he probably would have been famous. Instead, the valiant effort of his troops and 1,200 African-Americans pressed into service from neighboring plantations failed, mainly because of a caprice of nature — the river level dropped several feet — and the limited dimensions of the canal that was all the work force, reduced by excessive heat and widespread disease, could construct.[1]

Williams abandoned his attempt to divert the Mississippi at Vicksburg, but Major General Ulysses S. Grant revived that project six months later, and it became known as Grant's Canal. The project again failed, not because of low river stages but, ironically, high stages along with insufficient equipment and Confederate countermeasures.[2]

To appreciate the plan, one only has to look at a map of the Mississippi River in the vicinity of Vicksburg as it was in 1862-63. At that time Vicksburg was situated on the outside of a sharp horseshoe bend in the river. Its position, on steep bluffs which met the river just at the bend and ran south about four miles before receding eastward from the

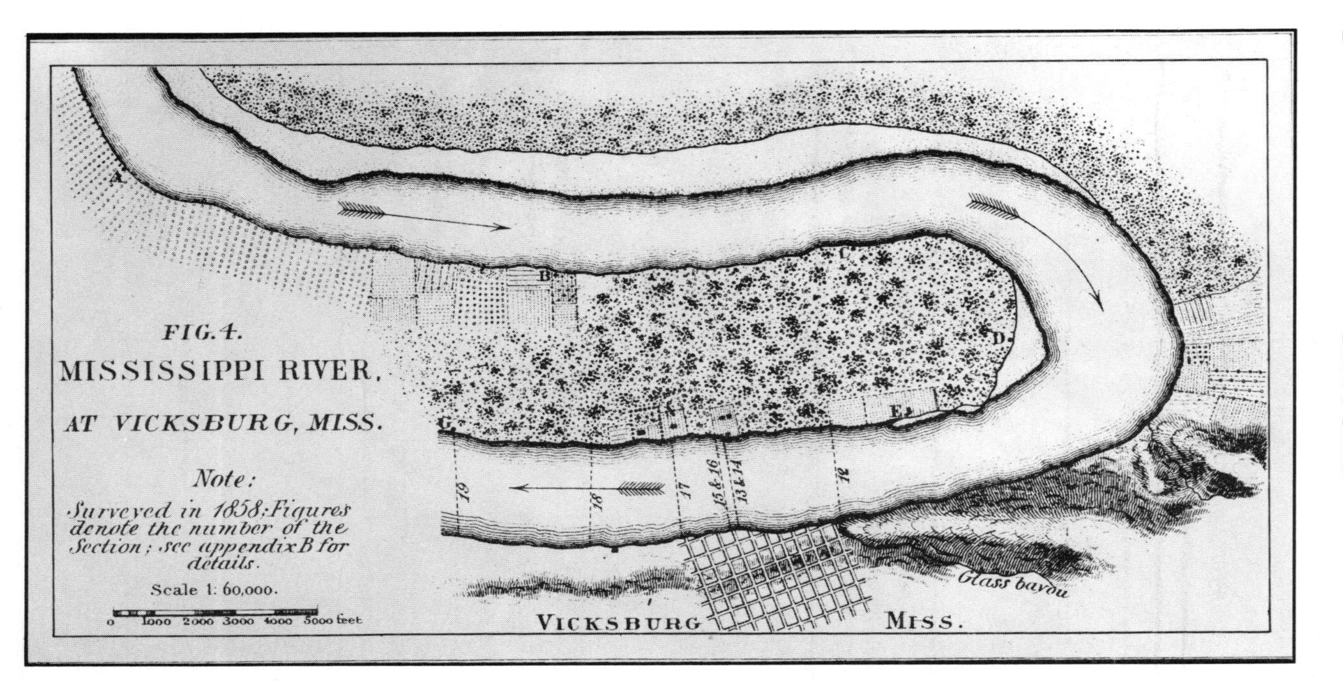


**1858 MAP SHOWING THE MISSISSIPPI RIVER AT VICKSBURG.**

*AUTHOR'S COLLECTION*

river, gave the city a commanding view of the river and the alluvial flatlands on either side to the west.

The Mississippi River was constantly changing course. Its meanderings produced horseshoe bends and it was not rare for those bends to become so narrow that ultimately the river cut across them, changing its channel and leaving the old channel an ox-bow lake. Such cutoffs or changes in the river's position could ruin the economic value of whatever bordered it.

The narrow neck of land just across from Vicksburg was known as De Soto Point. In 1853 it had been identified by a nationally prominent civil engineer, Charles Ellet, Jr., as a likely location for a natural cutoff.[3] Fearing the economic consequences of such an event, Vicksburgers were responsible for the state legislature's passing a bill in 1858 outlawing efforts which, in any way, could result in a cutoff.[4] In 1862, Union forces decided to break that law.

* * *

The South was still intact at the end of the first year of the Civil War. Consequently, the Union devised a strategy to cut the Confederacy in two by taking control of the Mississippi River. That would both cut off Confederate supply sources from the west and facilitate the deployment of Union troops. Special ironclad gunboats and rams were built to attack Confederate fortifications and river vessels. In January 1862 a combined army and navy operation began reducing fortified positions on the lower end of the Tennessee and Cumberland rivers and in early March the first of the Confederate fortified positions on the Mississippi River fell as the Union began working downstream.

Vicksburg was one of half a dozen towns along the Mississippi River of commercial importance. Militarily, it was the most strategic in that it also was connected to a railroad from both the east and the west. The railroad from Jackson connected to Vicksburg and a ferry connected Vicksburg to the just completed link of the Vicksburg, Shreveport and Texas Railroad which reached westward to Monroe, Louisiana.

In April 1862 the Confederate military realized that Vicksburg would have to be defended. At the time they thought an attack would come from upriver, but surprisingly, it came from below the city.[5] Although there were defenses on the river below New Orleans — Forts Jackson and St. Philip — there was little concern over a naval attack coming up the river from the Gulf of Mexico. The lack of concern grew out of Confederate President Jefferson Davis's, who had been the U.S. Secretary of War under President Franklin Pierce, awareness of the continual problems of maintaining navigation across the bars at the passes entering the Mississippi. With dredging discontinued after 1860, as a result of secession, the Confederacy felt relatively secure against attack from deep draft ocean warships which might attempt to enter the river from the Gulf, especially some 450 river miles up the Mississippi at Vicksburg. However, during March 1862, Flag Officer David G. Farragut, commanding the West Gulf Blockading Squadron, was able to pass all but one of his ships over the bar guarding the entrance to the river, but not without having to resort to towing. New Orleans fell April 25, 1862. In less than a month, a joint army and navy expedition was at Vicksburg demanding its surrender.

Seven hastily thrown-up earthwork batteries, comprising eighteen guns, were spread along the bluffs and waterfront in anticipation as Farragut's advance fleet arrived south of Vicksburg on May 18, 1862.[6] New Orleans, Baton Rouge and Natchez had all surrendered without a shot. No town along the river had dared to resist Farragut's fleet. However, Vicksburg was the first fortified city the Union navy encountered. Vicksburg's mayor had even brashly refused a demand for her surrender.[7]

Despite the arrival of the remainder of Farragut's river expedition fleet and a small army contingent, the resolve of the Rebels did not change. After a week of cautiously feeling out the Vicksburg defenses, Farragut withdrew to New Orleans, leaving a few ships immediately downstream from the city to curtail enemy movements on the river.

Farragut met with Major General Benjamin Butler, who had assumed command of New Orleans after its surrender. The question was how to conquer Vicksburg, the southern terminus of a 350-mile segment of the Mississippi River

**VICKSBURG FROM DE SOTO POINT, JULY 1862.**

*HARPER'S WEEKLY, AUGUST 2, 1862*

extending up to Memphis still under Confederate control. The Department of the Navy wanted Vicksburg conquered or reduced, it didn't matter which. The Farragut-Butler plan was well conceived, complete with alternative strategies. First, Farragut was to make the torturous 300-mile return trip upstream against the mighty Mississippi with his ocean-going warships.[8] Since his fleet alone was insufficient for conquering Vicksburg in May, Farragut ordered Commodore David D. Porter to send his mortar schooners to Vicksburg from the Gulf of Mexico. Farragut hoped that the mortars could flatten Vicksburg by arcing their 200-pound bombs onto the town from the river below. But even if Union guns could destroy Vicksburg, it was control or reduction of the Rebel batteries that really mattered. Troops would be necessary to go ashore and capture the guns. To accomplish this, Farragut was accompanied by 3,000 troops under Williams.

If Farragut could not accomplish his task by conventional military methods, Vicksburg, as he and Butler believed, could be neutralized by divorcing her from the river. They reasoned that by digging a canal across the base of De Soto Point, the Mississippi could be enticed to take the shortcut permanently. After all, it was only three-quarters of a mile across versus ten miles around by the natural channel. With these plans Farragut, Porter and Williams proceeded upriver to Vicksburg.[9]

Secretary of War, Edwin M. Stanton, received Butler's report outlining the planned operations against Vicksburg. The idea of constructing a cutoff to divert the river away from Vicksburg, which would allow Union vessels to bypass the guns on the bluffs at Vicksburg, impressed Stanton. He responded, "Your suggestion in regard to Vicksburg is one of great importance, apparently easy of execution and would be productive of very important results. If your force is strong enough, or if General Halleck could cooperate with you, there could be no doubt of its success."[10]

Stanton viewed the cutoff as a bloodless solution to eliminating the last Confederate point of control on the Mississippi, but not wanting to leave anything to chance, he wrote Halleck who was in Corinth, Mississippi, urging him to participate in the project. However, Halleck could not spare any troops.[11]

Stanton apparently passed on his report from Butler to the Secretary of the Navy, Gideon Welles, who in turn wrote

Flag Officer Charles H. Davis, Commander of U.S. Naval Forces of the Mississippi. Davis was in Memphis repairing his ironclads after having captured the town and destroying Confederate naval forces there in early June. Welles acquainted Davis with the cutoff, "The Department desires to call your attention to the narrow neck of land opposite Vicksburg, formed by a bend in the Mississippi River, the width of which is not more than three-quarters of a mile. The water flows over this, and it is thought by opening a ditch the river will soon force a channel through, sufficient for purpose of navigation, and thus obviate the necessity of passing Vicksburg. As soon as practical, you should examine the feasibility of this measure."[12]

On June 25, Williams's troops landed and set up camp on the Louisiana shore about three miles below Vicksburg. They were part of a force which included 17 of Porter's mortar boats and steamers, and 12 gunboats and 3 sloops under Farragut. Just above the bend was Lieutenant Colonel Alfred W. Ellet's* ram fleet fresh from their June 6 victory at Memphis while Commodore Charles H. Davis's gunboats were still on their way from Memphis. Only De Soto Point separated Farragut's fleet from Ellet's, and only the guns of Vicksburg could enforce this separation. The proposed cutoff could join these fleets by allowing them to bypass those guns, and give the Union total control of the Mississippi River.

Williams initiated the cutoff planned earlier in the month. After selecting the location for the canal**, the surveying, clearing and excavating one and one-third miles of land straight across the base of De Soto Point (well out of range of the guns at Vicksburg) began. The slope of the projected waterway would be much greater than the natural course and, once complete, gravity would propel the water across the peninsula rather than around it. The goal of the Union army engineers was to change the course of the magnificent and mighty Mississippi River.

The cutoff began with optimism among the troops. Slaves or contraband, as they were called, were procured from the

---

* brother of Charles Ellet, Jr. and commander of the Army's ram fleet.

** Willams did not choose the shortest distance across the peninsula because that route was too close to the existing batteries at Vicksburg.

**WILLIAMS'S TROOPS LANDING OPPOSITE VICKSBURG. ALTHOUGH THE SKETCH WAS MADE BY AN OFFICER IN THE EXPEDITION, THERE WERE NO HILLS ON THE LOUISIANA SIDE.**

*FRANK LESLIE'S, JULY 26, 1862*

**CONFISCATED SLAVES WORKING ON THE CUTOFF.**

*HARPER'S WEEKLY, AUGUST 2, 1862*

surrounding countryside to do the labor, but because the canal was a fall back alternative plan, Farragut went ahead with his initial plans to silence the fortifications at Vicksburg.

On June 27, the navy pounded Vicksburg with mortar shells. But despite Porter's best efforts, they could not set Vicksburg aflame.[13] During the pre-dawn hours of the 28th, Farragut churned upriver with his gunboats and sloops. But by that time the Rebels had increased their number of batteries to at least 11, mounting a total of 29 guns.[14] A tremendous duel took place between the floating batteries of Farragut and the land batteries of Vicksburg. When the smoke cleared, neither side could claim victory. Eight of Farragut's ships had passed around the bend to safety above Vicksburg and none of his vessels were sunk, although they suffered a total of 30 hits resulting in 16 deaths and 28 casualties. That engagement led Union forces to conclude that Vicksburg was not to be taken by a naval force alone.[15]

As a result of that failure, the cutoff took on greater importance. More black laborers from surrounding plantations were pressed into labor gangs digging the cutoff. Theodore R. Davis, a war correspondent for *Harper's Weekly* reported optimistically: "...our men are busy cutting a canal through the neck of land, which will have the effect of ruining the city, as it will be the means of changing the course of the river. This the people have been fearful of for some time, for by doing so Vicksburg is soon left an inland town forever. The river soon permanently changes its course."[16]

Commodore Davis finally arrived at De Soto Point with four of his gunboats and six mortars. He inspected Williams's efforts on the peninsula and responded to Welles's directive concerning the cutoff. "The Department will already have learned with pleasure that the proposed cut has been commenced. I am informed by General Williams that the ditch will be finished tomorrow." However, he gave a sobering premonition of the future by noting that the river was falling rapidly.[17]

By July 4, 1,200 blacks augmented Williams's troops.[18] Despite the falling river and the delay in completion of the cutoff, success seemed certain to Davis. In fact he seemed

**SKETCH OF VICKSBURG SHOWING HER BEING SHELLED FROM THE RIVER.**

*HARPER'S WEEKLY, MAY 16, 1863*

**MAP SHOWING FARRAGUT'S ENGAGEMENT WITH AND PASSAGE OF THE GUNS OF VICKSBURG ON JUNE 28, 1862.**

*ORN 18:598*

**KEY TO MAP**

**A** HILL BATTERIES, 300 FEET HIGH, 1,500 YARDS FROM THE WATER, 20 GUNS.

**B** WATER BATTERY, 5 GUNS.

**C** WATER BATTERY, 3 GUNS.

**D** VICKSBURG, BUILT ON SIDE OF SLOPE RISING 300 FEET.

**V** COURT HOUSE, PUBLIC BUILDING, CHURCHES, ETC., AREA NOT FORTIFIED.

**E** TERRACED BATTERIES, ABOVE EACH OTHER.

**F** BATTERY.

**G** MORTAR FLEET, DISTANCE 4,000 FEET.

**H** *HARTFORD.*

**R** *RICHMOND.*

**BK** *BROOKLYN.*

**I** ORDER OF BATTLE AND ADVANCE.

**K** TURNING PLACE OF SQUADRON.

**L** TRACK OF VESSELS THAT RAN THE BATTERIES AND ANCHORED UPSTREAM AROUND THE POINT AMONG THE GUNBOATS.

**M** *BROOKLYN, KATAHDIN* AND *KENNEBEC* ENGAGING ENEMY FOR 2 HOURS AND 40 MINUTES.

**N** *BROOKLYN* AT ANCHOR NEAR THE MORTAR FLEET AFTER THE ACTION.

intoxicated with the idea of its success as he wrote a lengthy official report.

> ...We require twenty thousand men, and perhaps more, to hold Vicksburg. But there is a method of turning all these heavy fortifications and batteries, and of chastising the insolent and corrupt city of Vicksburg, that seems to have been provided by Nature herself...It has always been a subject of apprehension to the religious and enlightened inhabitants of that hell (as gambling houses are termed in Paris) lest the channel of the river should of its own accord, or by artificial means, take its way across the narrow neck, and thus annihilate Vicksburg by converting the site of the town into the bottom of a shute [branch channel] instead of the bank of the main channel bordering on deep water...Now General Williams has so far advanced in cutting the ditch that it will be completed tomorrow night.[19]

Once again, Davis left the door open for failure noting:

> It is not a propitious moment for the undertaking, because the river is falling. It is the rising river, the swell and flood of the freshet, that force open these new channels, after the hard-pan below the soil has been removed and the way opened to the loose sand underlying it. But though the river is now falling at this place, there is promise of a speedy return of the waters. It is reported that the June rise is great, and the rains heavy on the upper Missouri, and that all the upper rivers are in good stage.[20]

The task of digging the ditch was miserable as men had to work when both the temperature and humidity topped 90 degrees and 90 percent, respectively. Their situation was made worse by inadequate rations and unpurified drinking water. Nor was a good night's rest assured as the soldiers were attacked by mosquitoes and enveloped by high, nighttime temperatures and humidity. The Missis-

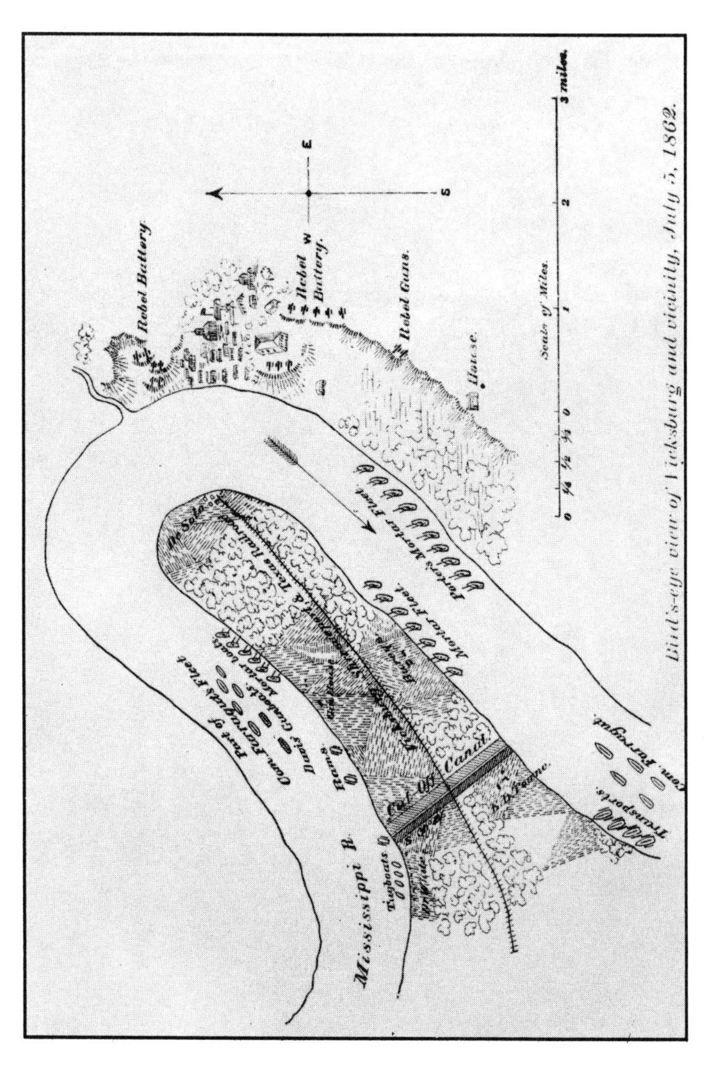

**JULY 5, 1862 MAP.**

*OR 15:29*

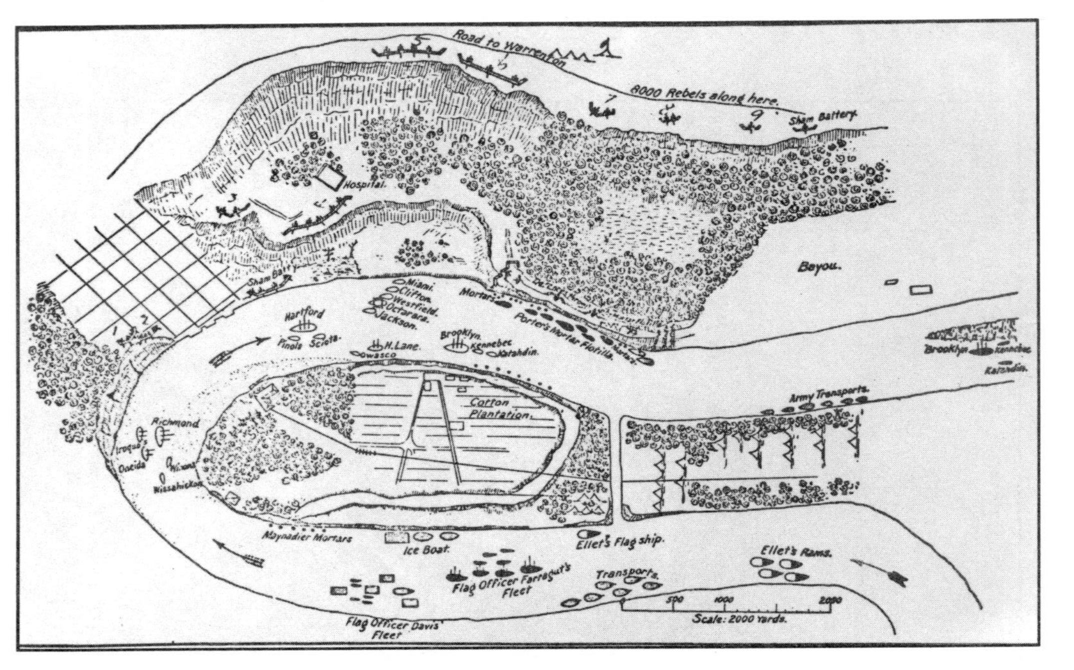


**MAP SHOWING FARRAGUT'S ENGAGEMENT ON JUNE 28 AND SUBSEQUENT POSITION ALONG WITH PORTER'S, DAVIS'S AND ELLET'S POSITIONS THROUGH JULY 10, 1862.**

*ORN 18:646*

sippi, too, did not seem a willing partner as she steadily dropped at a rate of almost a foot per day.

The days wore on, punctuated only by occasional shelling aimed at Vicksburg by the mortar boats. The backbreaking toil of digging the cutoff continued without let up. Despite stifling heat, rapidly spreading sickness, and a falling river, guarded optimism prevailed because news had come from St. Louis that the river was rising![21]

By July 6, no rise had come. Instead the river continued dropping. After a week and a half of hard labor, the bottom of the ditch was still above the river. Optimism began to fade.

On July 10, Porter headed downstream to the Gulf. Although he had been ordered to take part of his mortar fleet to Hampton Roads, Virginia, his departure was a moral victory to the defenders of Vicksburg. Farragut, too, wished to leave for fear the rapidly dropping river stage would strand his fleet until the annual spring floods.[22]

The next day speculation brewed into excitement when Williams solicited Commodore Davis's help in an experiment to open the cutoff. Davis was a supporter of the project and still held hope long after his naval colleagues had lost theirs. He wrote in his log:

> No change has taken place in the state of affairs here since I wrote last, except that the canal is cut and the attempt is to be made to open it this afternoon. The river has fallen continually, with slight pauses, since our arrival, but it is hoped that by putting sternwheel steamers at the opening on this side, the sides and bottom may be washed in, and the river may be persuaded to enter into its new channel. It is a rather big undertaking, but there is a good deal of faith somewhere. It is again said, in the *Missouri Republican* of the 6th inst., that the Missouri River is rising from its source to the mouth, and that the upper end of the river is very high. One of my oldest and most experienced pilots says that there will be a "big river" (such is the phrase) in ten days or a fortnight. Should this prove to be the case, we shall

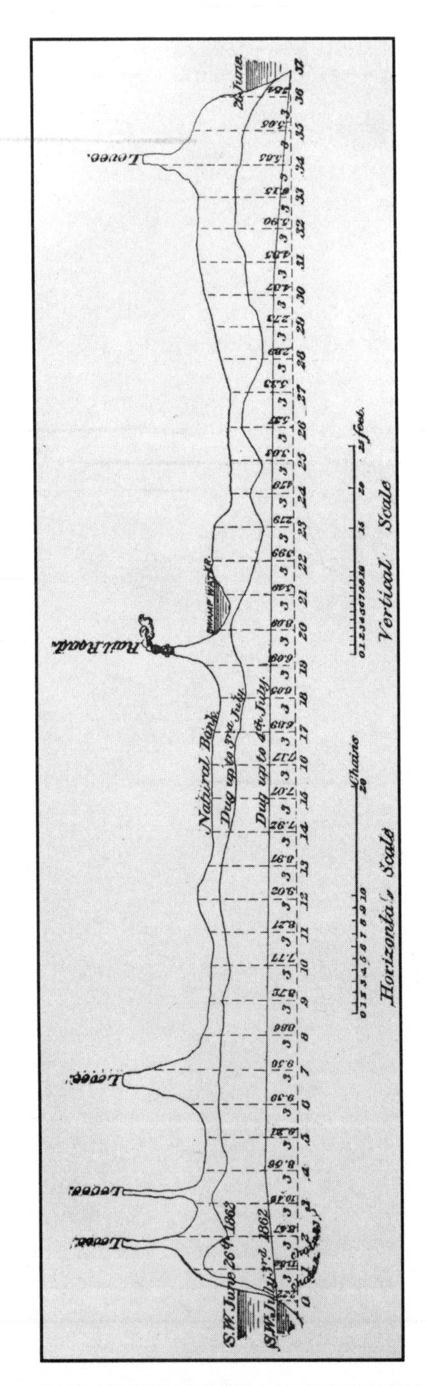


OR 15:30

**PROFILE OF THE CANAL ACROSS DE SOTO POINT.**

soon know what the Father of Waters has to say to this attempt to stay and divert his course.[23]

Davis's experiment with the steamers failed and failures have their critics. Not the least bit flattering to Yankee engineering, a correspondent for the *Chicago Tribune* wrote this derisive article about the cutoff:

> It is not a canal, but simply a ditch. When we arrived here it had been completed only through that portion of the neck which is inside of the levee, or embankment, to prevent the river's overflow. It was then about fifteen feet wide, and three, or three and a half feet deep. This, it was supposed, was of sufficient depth to allow the water of the river to flow through, but when the levee at each end of it was cut through, it was found to be above the level of the water. The river had fallen some during the process of digging, but not enough to account for so great a shortcoming.
> The mountain would not come to Mohammed and some wiseacre determined to make it come by placing an old stern-wheel boat at the lower side of the entrance to the canal, to work her wheel, and so paddle the water up into it, which succeeded in wetting the bottom of the canal just enough to make it muddy, but no more. This experiment of making water run up hill not proving very successful, it was determined to deepen the ditch. The bottom being, as I said before, about fifteen feet wide, the one half of this bottom, longitudinally, was dug five feet deeper, the entire length of the canal, the earth being thrown up on the other half of the original bottom, and so that a transverse section of the canal would show like this:

> By this means a small thread of water, about a foot wide, was decoyed into it, where it remains at present, looking very much bewildered, as though it did not know where to run to. The entire (east) side of the canal is now composed of loose earth, thrown up from the deepening, and should the river rise sufficient to make a current through the canal, I think the loose earth would be undermined by the current, and coming down would soon fill it up sufficiently to stop the current. The labor of widening the canal would almost be equal to that of digging a new one.[24]

It is hard to say whether the reporter had been influenced by cynical Union officers that had given up on the canal idea or whether he was simply amused by the episode. However, military officers have to report their failures in a more contrite setting. Thus, Williams briefly described his failure:

> Up to the 11th our prospects were promising that the canal...would succeed...the general grade of the bottom...had been carried about $1^1/_2$ feet below the level of the Mississippi, and in some twelve hours would have been ready to let in the water, when suddenly caving began at several points and so delayed the work, that the end of three days found us some feet above the level of the river.[25]

The cutoff effort was just one in a series of failures for the Union at Vicksburg. Three days after that embarrassing experiment, the as yet uncompleted Confederate ram *Arkansas* steamed out of the Yazoo River and on into the Mississippi River twelve miles above Vicksburg, turned downstream and ran through Farragut's, Davis's and Ellet's fleets to the safety of the Vicksburg wharf. Nature was extracting her toll also, although impartially, as both sides suffered tremendous sickness.

The river had fallen an estimated 25 feet since Farragut's arrival in May.[26] He was impatient to leave. More worried than ever that the falling river would strand his fleet, he once again reminded Welles of his fleet's precarious situation as he had in his frequent official status reports.

The heat and humidity of July continued unabated. While Washington deliberated on a course of action against Vicksburg, Williams, in recognition that Vicksburg could not be taken by his present force, proposed a grand enlargement of the canal:

> ...we have encountered at least temporary failure after great labor and some anxiety. If not interrupted by the rebels, nor stopped by orders from headquarters, it is my purpose to cut a real canal, to the depth of the lowest fall of the river, here say some 40 to 45 feet, which work will employ 3,000 negroes for 3 months.

He concluded his report by trying to claim something positive about the canal, "Happily the excavation we have made is a mighty ditch, and the earth thrown up a respectable parapet which can be turned to military purposes if necessary."[27]

Williams did not get far with his grand canal idea. Due to sickness, he could only muster about 700 of his original force of 3,200. In addition, many of the confiscated slaves were also afflicted. The project came to an end by the 21st after he received orders to return to Baton Rouge.[28]

A correspondent for the *New York Tribune* described the seriousness:

> The sickness on the "Flotilla" continued to increase and nearly every vessel bears the appearance of a hospital. The weather is so hot and sultry that no one can sleep under cover and when men lie in the open air they incur disease from the malaria in the atmosphere. General Williams's troops have suffered terribly as many graves on the Louisiana Point attest.

Sickness was so prevalent that treating it had exhausted both Williams's and Farragut's entire stock of medicine.[29] When the Union forces withdrew from Vicksburg on July 24, only about half were fit for duty.[30]

Shortly after the Union had left, curiosity drew a Rebel scouting party to cross the river to inspect the abandoned encampment and ditch. They found an estimated 600 graves testifying to ravages of disease. Although the Union had attempted to return the confiscated slaves to their owners, about 500 were found "most of them sick and all left in the woods without anything to eat or any provision whatever being made for them." [31]

* * *

Farragut and his fleet escorted Williams and his troops on board river transports down to Baton Rouge. Observers were shocked by the appearance of the troops as they unloaded at the waterfront. One of the Union soldiers who had been left behind to guard Baton Rouge noted, "There had been no battle in which he (Williams) had been engaged, but his troops looked as if they had come on furlough from Death himself."[32] But those troops indeed had not been in a battle, instead they had been engaged in manually digging a canal across De Soto Point.

After seeing Williams to Baton Rouge, Farragut continued on to New Orleans. The trip downstream from Vicksburg for his deep-draft, ocean-going warships was extremely risky. Besides not having Mississippi River pilots, the river, which had dropped faster than the troops could dig, continued to drop rapidly through the month of July. During falling stages, the natural channel shifts its course daily and the "crossings" (the stretch of river between the bends) become more shallow. Had any of Farragut's deeper draft ships run aground, they would have had to have been abandoned.

* * *

The reason that the cutoff failed was simply that the Mississippi River dropped faster than the canal could be dug. Had Williams not delayed leaving Baton Rouge, while the river stages were higher, perhaps the cutoff may have succeeded.

In mid July, after realizing that he had failed, Williams planned to enlarge the cross section. That ambitious effort was thwarted by sickness which had affected his forces even more than it did the naval forces. By that time, about 75 percent of his troops were on the sick list. If the enlargement had been accomplished, then the next high water might possibly have resulted in the river changing course. Ironically Charles Ellet, Jr., who had predicted the cutoff in 1853 when under contract by the U.S. Government to survey the Mississippi, was mortally wounded at Memphis while commanding the Ram Fleet, otherwise, he would have been at De Soto Point in June and may have played an important role in the cutoff project.

* * *

With the departure of the Union forces, Vicksburg remained the only town of consequence on the Mississippi not under Union control. The Confederates knew that it was only a matter of time before the Federals would return for another confrontation but they could not afford the luxury of maintaining a large, armed force at Vicksburg in anticipation. Instead, only a small garrison remained behind (Major General Earl Van Dorn dispatched Major General John C. Breckinridge to Baton Rouge in late July and Van Dorn departed for north Mississippi in early September).

Preparations were made for the Yankee's return. New batteries were built and ammunition was stockpiled. The Confederates did not attach enough significance to Williams's attempted cutoff to consider filling it in. But they did clear the timber on De Soto Point to allow them to fire across it so that Union vessels would not be as protected should they return.[33]

After the withdrawal of the Federal fleets in July, the Mississippi River was relatively open to Confederate usage between Baton Rouge and Vicksburg (the Union riverboats still patrolled the river above Vicksburg). The city on the bluffs was still the only strategic location capable of preventing Union control of the river.

The importance to the Confederacy of still controlling Vicksburg and the 250 miles of river below is partially illustrated by the observations of a Rebel soldier stationed in Vicksburg. In October he noted:

> Our rations were scant and we had to hire them cooked. Various duties fell to my lot on this detail. Perhaps the most disagreeable was guarding a boat laden with coal at the water's edge on cold, dark windy nights. While occupying the position one day, I saw a herd of Texas cattle, five hundred in number, swim across the River. They were driven in apparently just opposite the city, but they were borne downstream by the current until the landing on the Eastward side was made about two miles below the city.[34]

Furthermore, she was designated by the two governments as a site for prisoner exchange.[35]

* * *

In October Grant was placed in charge of the Department of the Tennessee, headquartered at Memphis, and Porter replaced Davis as commander of the Western Flotilla, renamed the Mississippi Squadron. Together, they were to take control of the Mississippi River and cut the South in two.

As Grant organized his campaign, the Confederates gathered at Vicksburg to await the assault. In December, Union troops moved south with Grant leading part of his army through the center of Mississippi, while Major General William T. Sherman led 32,000 troops down the river on 60 transports. They were accompanied by Acting Rear Admiral David D. Porter* and his fleet which included about 50 armored and supporting vessels mounting over 300 guns.

Five days before Christmas, Van Dorn's Confederate cavalry swung behind Grant's column, destroying his sup-

---

* Who had been promoted since participating in the summer campaign.

ply base at Holly Springs, Mississippi. As a result, Grant withdrew back to Memphis, leaving Vicksburg to Sherman.

The previous summer's expedition against Vicksburg had shown that direct assault from the river would be fruitless, therefore Sherman had the transports navigate up the Yazoo River above Vicksburg. There, the battle of Chickasaw Bayou took place on December 27–29 and Union forces were repulsed and withdrew.

While Sherman's troops left the vicinity of Vicksburg to attack Fort Hindman at Arkansas Post on the Arkansas River, part of Porter's fleet remained to harass the Rebels. Meanwhile, members of the United States Coast Survey reconnoitered the area making a survey of the river and Rebel gun locations.[36]

* * *

Grant had to find a location to get his troops onto the east bank of the river in order to attack Vicksburg from land. Ascending the Yazoo River was the most logical route but he ruled it out for several reasons. First, the Confederates had mined the river, resulting in the sinking of the U.S. ironclad *Cairo* in mid-December. In addition a "raft" of floating logs chained to the banks blocked the navigable channel leading to Yazoo City.[37] And finally, bluffs commanded any potential landing spots as Sherman had learned.

To get above Yazoo City required penetrating the Mississippi "Delta", the local name for the vast, alluvial lowlands between Memphis on the north and Vicksburg on the south, flanked by the Mississippi River on the west and the steep loess bluffs on the east. The annual winter rains had already bloated the Yazoo and her tributaries causing vast flooding which precluded any land movement across the Delta. However, Grant allowed Lieutenant Colonel George Wilson to lead a riverine assault through the narrow channels of the Coldwater and Tallahatchie rivers into the Yazoo River. Grant did not pin much hope on this "Yazoo Pass Expedition" although he did commit a large force to the project. He was concerned, and rightly so, that the Rebels would find out in time to prepare adequate defenses.

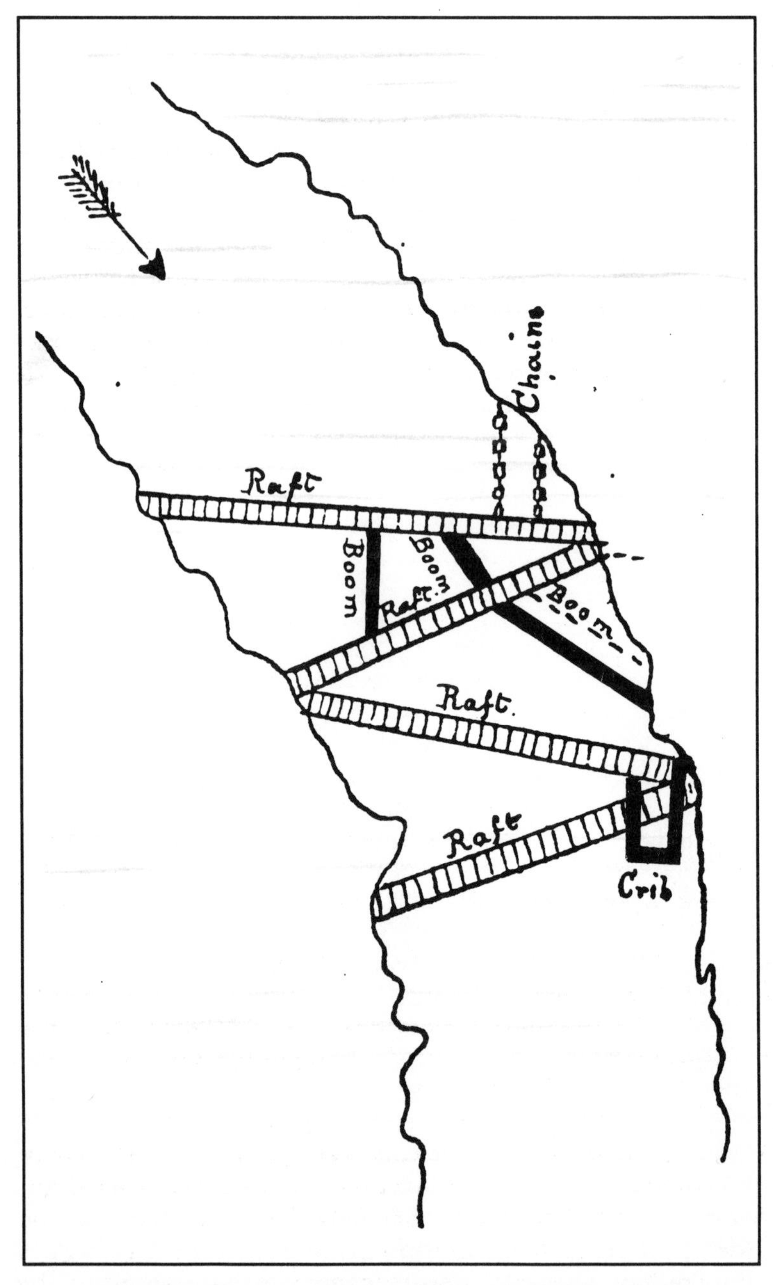


**CONFEDERATE RAFT BLOCKING NAVIGATION ON YAZOO RIVER.**

*ORN 24:712*

There were three ways to get below Vicksburg. The most obvious, and normally the easiest, was to march through Louisiana, but the winter rains and resultant flooding made the roads impassible for moving a large army and necessary supplies. Besides, this plan would require his transports to run past the guns at Vicksburg in order to reach his troops and carry them across to the east bank. An alternative was to ferry troops and supplies through the myriad of Louisiana bayous, down the Red River and then up the Mississippi River. This would require the procurement of a great number of small paddlewheelers of the Ohio River class as well as digging a connecting channel from the Mississippi, above Vicksburg, to the first bayou. The final choice was to revive Williams's cutoff. That decision was, in part, because of pressure from President Lincoln who was a proponent of this project.[38]

Grant had around 45,000 troops at his disposal. In mid January they moved down river and most camped along the Louisiana shore between Vicksburg and Lake Providence. Grant was prepared for a long campaign and the cutoff was to be an integral part of his scheme.

* * *

On January 10, 1863 Grant, still in Memphis, ordered Colonel Josiah W. Bissell, who had been in charge of constructing a bypass around Island No. 10 the previous March, to survey Williams's cutoff and recommend new work.[39] Williams's efforts of the previous summer showed few signs of deterioration when army engineers surveyed the attempted cutoff. The ditch, as they found it, was between nine and twelve feet wide and little more than six feet deep with trees and stumps cluttering the slopes.[40]

As protection against enemy artillery and possible attack, Williams had had all the diggings thrown to the east or Vicksburg side of the ditch. In one respect this was fortunate, because the canal obviously required widening and deepening and, with the previously excavated material all on one side, it would be easier to widen the project. Furthermore, the west side of the canal needed a levee to confine the waters to the canal and keep them out of the camps.

Williams had noted that the downstream end of his effort was commanded by bluffs well back off the river. He was concerned that despite the distance, rifled shells could reach the canal. He was also concerned because the orientation of the canal was perpendicular to the line of bluffs which would allow the Vicksburg guns to enfilade the canal.[41]

Although Williams reported his concerns to Washington during the summer of 1862, they had not been passed onto Grant. It was not until January 19, when Welles wrote to Porter that the location and orientation of the canal was officially questioned:

> The President is exceedingly anxious that a canal from which practical and useful results would follow should be cut through the peninsula opposite Vicksburg.
>
> If a canal were cut at a higher point up the river than the first one, as you some time since suggested, so as to catch the current before it has made the curve, and also to avoid the bluffs below the city, it would probably be a success. The Department desires that this plan be tried whenever you deem it expedient and can have cooperation of the army.[42]

On the same day that Welles sent his directive to Porter, Grant had steamed half way to Vicksburg from Memphis where he met with Porter, Sherman, and Major General John McClernand to discuss strategy. After the meeting, Grant wrote to his superior, Major General Henry W. Halleck, about a new location for the cutoff:

> I propose running a canal through, starting far enough above the old one commenced last summer, to receive the stream where it impinges against the shore with the greatest velocity. The old canal left the river in an eddy, and in a line perpendicular to this stream, and also to the crest of hills opposite, with a battery directed against the outlet. This new canal will debouch below the bluffs on the opposite side of the river, and give our gunboats a fair chance against any fortifications that may be placed to oppose them.[43]

* * *

The Mississippi River was at flood stage in January and still rising. With rain almost daily and a high and rising river, it was difficult for Sherman's XV Corps and McClernand's XIII Corps to disembark from the transports onto the levee at Young's Point, a few miles upstream from Williams's ditch. Nonetheless, thousands of troops landed, sloshed through the mud and set up camp.

The reappearance of Union forces caused quite a stir in Vicksburg. A Confederate reporter wrote:

> This has been a lively day here, caused by the appearance of a large number of the enemy's fleet near the cut-off canal. All day transports have been busy bringing down troops and landing them about a mile and a half above that point. Camp fires have been visible along the levee, and large squads of enemy could be seen with a glass, maneuvering about the canal. White's field is dotted tents and troops were perceptible along the river, in front of Dr. Young's place.
>
> About twenty transports were fastened on the Louisiana bank, and one was on guard on the Mississippi shore opposite White's cotton gin...About noon an iron clad gunboat took position below the transports. They are evidently concentrating a large force near their old camp ground. Our lower guns have fired occasionally during the day, with what effects is unknown.
>
> They doubtless design another effort at the Canal, but they will have to go through an average depth of 20 feet of blue clay for two miles before the father of waters will co-operate in the nefarious experiment. In the meantime, their labor may be disturbed.[44]

The landing of troops went on for weeks. As the river inched its way up, only the levees kept the waters of the

Mississippi out of the campgrounds. Because the water table was so high, mule teams trying to pull wagon loads of equipment anywhere but along the levees often would come to a halt as the wagons sank to their axles.[45]

Steamers lined the banks as far as the eye could see, ready to board the troops in case the levees failed.[46] Crevasses (or breaks in the levee) had already occurred some miles up and downstream from the campsites.[47] The levees were 15 to 20 feet high with crowns of about the same dimensions and served as roadways as well as flood protection.[48]

On January 23, 1863, troops were detailed to enlarge the canal rather than construct a new one as Welles and Porter and Grant and Halleck had already agreed.[49] But because their correspondence does not address the decision or discuss options for enlarging the existing canal, one can only speculate. Perhaps they chose the enlargement because Williams's ditch already existed and the rapidly rising river gave prospects of quick success, whereas to dig a new route would require more tools than were presently available. Thus McClernand directed his troops to continue what Williams had previously started.

The river had already encroached about 75 yards into the upper end of the canal and surface water stood in pools throughout the entire length.[50] By the next day there was close to two feet of water flowing through the canal due to the rise in the river.[51] Even though the water impeded digging, officers hoped that the erosive power of the current would enlarge the canal naturally.[52] To aid nature, soldiers were directed to dig pits along the canal with hopes of speeding the erosion process. Although by the end of the week the ditch was an average of sixteen feet wide with about five feet of water flowing in it, it showed no signs of enlarging itself through washing out the banks and eroding the bottom of the ditch.[53] McClernand, determined that the canal needed more water, reenacted a scene from the previous summer by having Porter send a sternwheeler to the upper entrance to push additional water into the canal, and like the previous summer, this again proved a failure.[54]

McClernand became so pessimistic that he began searching for alternate routes through the myriad of bayous

**TROOPS LANDING AT YOUNG'S POINT.**

*FRANK LESLIE'S, APRIL 4, 1863*

**VIEW OF UNION VESSELS (PADDLEWHEEL TRANSPORTS, TUG, MORTAR BOATS AND GUNBOATS) FROM ENCAMPMENTS ABOVE VICKSBURG.**

*FRANK LESLIE'S, MARCH 28, 1863*

and sloughs.[55] Sherman, too, expressed doubts for the success of the project and noted, "I have never seen men work more grudgingly."[56] Grant passed this pessimism onto Halleck, in Washington.[57] The feelings of the generals filtered down to their men and one soldier wrote, "There is a force at work making it wider but I do not think it will work and judging from the way the force is at work on it, I do not think our generals expect to make it work."[58]

However, the Federals did not give up on the project. Instead, they gave it undivided leadership in the form of an engineer. On January 28, Captain Frederick E. Prime, Corps of Engineers, was placed in charge of the canal effort. Up to this point, the project had suffered from haphazard leadership. He established his office aboard the steamer *Magnolia* which provided shelter for him to plan engineering activities for both the canal and levee repair.[59]

The ditch had to be widened. The rising river had provided water to flow through the canal, but it did not accomplish the anticipated scour. Despite a good gradient, the cross section was too small and too irregular resulting in insufficient velocity to erode the sides and bottom of the canal any appreciable degree.[60] Therefore a 10-foot widening was begun. But the soldiers could only dig that portion two and one half to four feet deep due to the water level in the canal. The efficient solution to the situation would have been to use a dredge and Prime requested one. But none was readily available. Grant had already dispatched Bissell, who he had previously ordered to survey Williams's effort, to St. Louis to obtain powder and tools for blasting and digging.

The location of the entrance of Williams's ditch was considered by some to be another problem. Steamboat captains criticized the location for being adjacent to an eddy which they claimed would preclude the cutoff from ever succeeding. So accepted was their view that Grant, who announced to Halleck ten days ago that he planned to move the canal, ordered Prime to cut a new entrance about 200 yards upstream.[61] The contraband help that Williams used were again gathered from the countryside, as they had been the previous summer, and put to work on the new entrance, where they began clearing the land and moving the earth.[62]

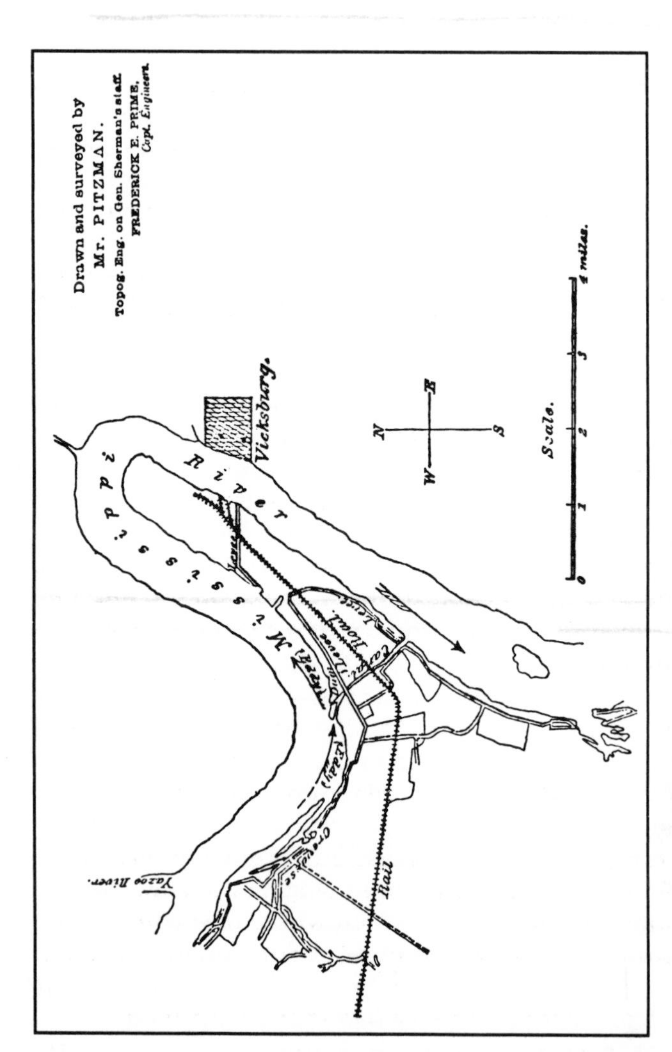


**MAP SHOWING LOCATION OF EDDY, CANAL AND LEVEES.**

*OR, PART I, 24:118*

The Confederates began to take the project seriously. The Vicksburg paper chastised the military for not having filled in Williams's ditch.[63] However, they did erect batteries opposite the lower end of the canal and, by February 16, were placing shells within the first 100 yards of the lower end.[64]

Grant did not share the Vicksburg editorial views. By February 4 he wrote that he had lost all faith in the cutoff and only continued the effort to avoid a negative press.[65] Sherman echoed these sentiments on the same day by writing, "This little affair of ours on Vicksburg Point is labor lost."[66]

Sherman noted in a letter to a friend that he feared that even if the canal succeeded in bypassing Vicksburg, it would not open the river as many had hoped. He believed that the Rebels would fortify other bluffs commanding a half dozen bends between Vicksburg and Baton Rouge. What he forgot was that to get below Vicksburg gave the Union the first access to high ground on the east bank since Memphis which would allow him to confront the defenders on land.[67]

However, Vicksburg with its more than 50 heavy caliber guns was impregnable to Union forces on the water and across the river. Porter illustrated Vicksburg's advantage over the navy:

> Vicksburg was by nature the strongest place on the river, but art has made it impregnable against floating batteries...The people in Vicksburg are the only ones who have yet hit upon the method of defending themselves against our gunboats, viz, not erecting water batteries, and placing the guns some distance back from the water, where they can throw a plunging shot, which none of our ironclads could stand.
>
> I mention these facts to show the Department that there is no possible hope of any success against Vicksburg by a gunboat attack or without an investment in the rear of the city by a large army. We can, perhaps, destroy the city and public buildings, but that would bring us no nearer the desired point (the

opening of the Mississippi) than we are now, and would likely put out the little spark of Union feeling still existing in Vicksburg.[68]

Sherman's views concerning the strategic importance of the canal were not shared by the Assistant Secretary of the Navy, Gustavus V. Fox, who, in a letter to Porter wrote:

> We wrote to you about cutting the canal further back. My impression is that it would be cheaper and better to set the whole army to work upon a new spot and turn the river clear of the hills and let Vicksburg go. I doubt whether the army can take it, and I do not see how you can do anything more than bombard it, which I would not do except for an object. The moment the canal is opened, away you go to Port Hudson...I dislike to see you all set down for a long siege at Vicksburg. The country cannot stand it at home or abroad. The President is of my opinion, that you better cut through farther back and do so at once.[69]

Despite Grant's and Sherman's negative assessments, Grant continued the project. He had already rerouted the canal entrance but not the lower half of the canal. Because no dredge was available, Prime decided that it would be best to close both the entrance and exit to the canal in order to drain it. Otherwise soldiers could not deepen it. Gunny sacks were filled with dirt and placed where the levees had previously been cut. Wooden framework helped serve as support. By February 9, they had secured the closures. Up to that time there had been a good current, and there was finally some evidence that the current had enlarged the canal (which had not been observed as recently as the previous week).[70]

In addition to plugging the entrance and exit to the canal and starting a new entrance, Prime ordered the raising of the canal levees. The lack of wheel barrows hampered the latter effort and the laborers could hardly keep pace with the rising water level. This was partially because the dams, constructed where levees previously crossed the ca-

**HEAD OF CUTOFF SHOWING CLOSURE.**

*FRANK LESLIE'S, MARCH 28, 1863*

nal, were relatively porous. By February 16, water in the canal had risen to within seven feet of the water level in the river. To help alleviate the situation, a hole was cut on the east side of the canal levee where there were no encampments. Soldiers worked around the clock strengthening the rest of the levees in order to protect their own campgrounds and prevent the project from failing.[71]

The 550 black laborers assigned to the new entrance section could only dig down four feet before hitting water. To lower the water table, the engineers constructed a sump in the upper end of the canal by driving wooden sheet piling. It was completed by February 9 and a steam pump was lowered into the pit to dewater that section. To their frustration, they couldn't get it to work until the 19th. Meanwhile, the new entrance was completed to a width of 60 feet and a depth of about 4 feet by the 12th.[72]

The weather, working in mud and living in unsanitary camp conditions took a heavy toll on the troops. Limited by lack of tools, only about 3,000 troops of the large available force were engaged on the canal. But those not having to perform "canal duty" did not escape the ravages of sickness. Diarrhea was common and many died. Of the roughly 35,000 soldiers camped along an 12-mile stretch from Young's Point north, about 85 died each day. As one soldier wrote, "The Spanish moss draped in the trees provided a mournful appearance to the soldiers as they listened to the daily death march of the fife and muffled drum and the report of the firing squad [for funerals] would be heard constantly from morning until night." The levees, being the only high ground, took on another function — they served as the burial grounds.[73]

The only real excitement in the vicinity of the canal occurred on the two occasions when Federal vessels ran past the batteries of Vicksburg. First, Colonel Charles Rivers Ellet* made a daring raid on the Vicksburg waterfront with the *Queen of the West* on February 2. Eleven days later, under the cover of darkness, the *Indianola* ran the batteries.

* Son of Charles Ellet, Jr.

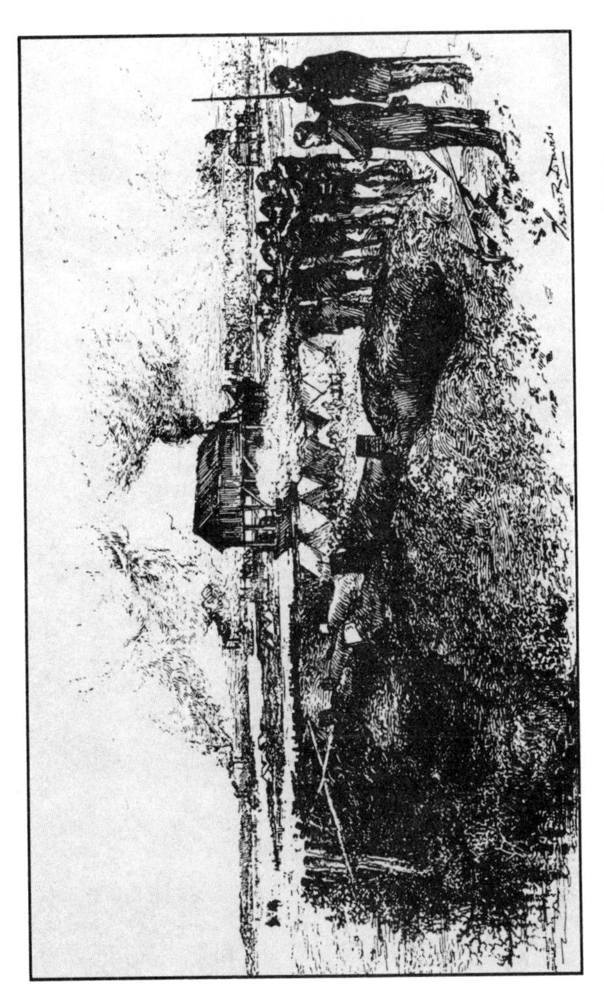

**FUNERAL ON THE LEVEE WITH THE MISSISSIPPI RIVER, CANAL AND DREDGES IN THE BACKGROUND.**

*BATTLES AND LEADERS 3:495*

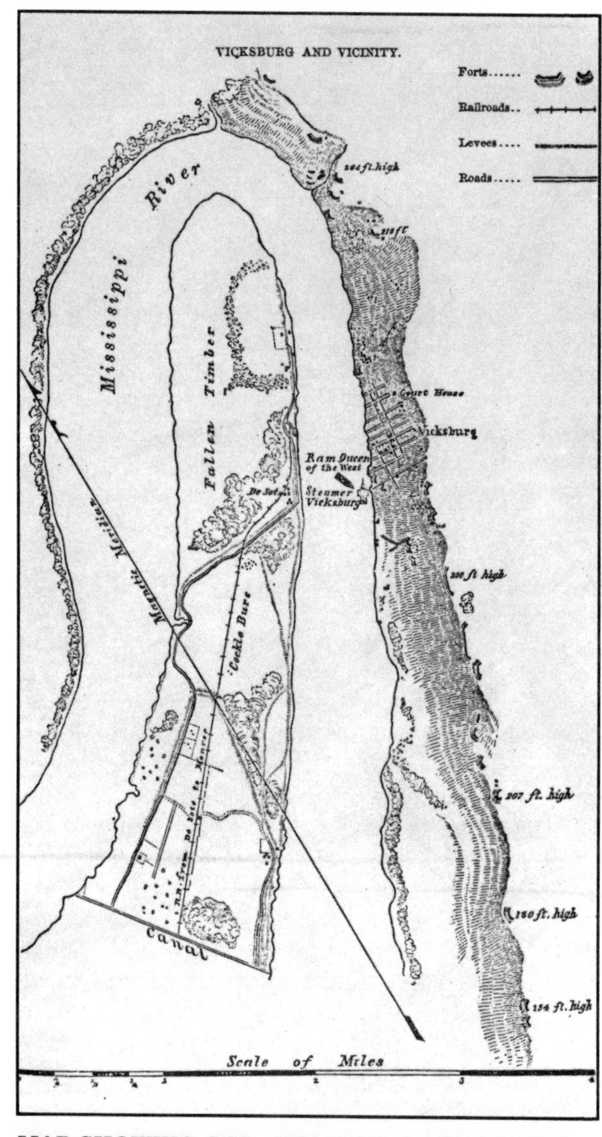


**MAP SHOWING COL. CHARLES RIVERS ELLET RAMMING THE STEAMER *VICKSBURG* AT THE WHARF AT VICKSBURG DURING THE NIGHT OF FEBRUARY 2, 1863. THE MAP ALSO SHOWS REBEL BATTERIES, CANAL AND LEVEES.**

*ORN 24:221*

By February 13, much of De Soto Point was flooded. Private Charles A. Willison of Company I, 76th Ohio, described the conditions.

> Rain and electric storms here were something terrific. [On February 14] the whole company were sent out on picket over night some 300 yards on the other side of the railroad. Rain fell in torrents most of the night and the lightning was fearful. While on picket post it was dangerous to carry our guns so we stuck them bayonet down into the ground and walked our beat some distance off. On return to the regiment in the morning found that lighting had struck a tent in Co B killing a couple non commissioned officers and injuring four others. Camp was flooded and everything soaked.[74]

Because the ground was so soggy and the levee so crowded, troops were now being shuttled from their camps to the project by steamer. In mid February work details were reorganized. Regiments, competing against each other, were each assigned 150-foot long segments of the canal. Each regiment was subdivided such that the soldiers only worked two hours a day on the canal.[75] Drilling, washing, cooking, gathering wood, and related activities consumed the rest of the duty time. Letters and diaries indicate a renewed enthusiasm despite working knee deep in mud and water.[76] Grant, in an about face, believed that the canal would be ready in two or three more weeks.[77]

On the 16th, Colonel George G. Pride, an aid to Grant, wired him from St. Louis announcing that he had secured two dredges and was negotiating for a third.*[78] Grant became more optimistic and wrote Halleck that the canal would be ready in 10 to 15 days.[79] The Vicksburg paper was also predicting a Yankee success.[80]

On the 19th, there was more good news as the steam pump began working in the new entrance.[81] Quickly drawing the water level down, it facilitated stump and dirt removal. Furthermore, a thousand black laborers were be-

* The names of the two dredges were the *Sampson* and *Hercules*. The names of the third and ultimately a fourth dredge are unknown.

ing brought down from Memphis to help.[82] The pump, however, could not keep all the water out of the canal, which greatly impeded its progress. Subsequently, the first of two dredges arrived on March 1, and on the 2nd began clearing an approach channel from the river to the levee to form the new entrance to the canal.[83]

To counter the guns opposite the lower end of the canal, Prime had batteries built at the canal's exit. What the Rebel shells could not do they hoped nature would as the March 2, 1863 edition of the *Vicksburg Whig* read, "The river at this point is rising quite rapidly again. We hope it will continue to swell until the Yankees across the river are drowned out like rats."

The military command in Vicksburg was convinced that even if the canal failed, Grant would succeed in moving his troops below Vicksburg and ultimately across the river to come in from behind. In anticipation they continued to fell timber, remove fences and erect earthwork fortifications around Vicksburg and now they contemplated erecting batteries at Grand Gulf.[84]

Union optimism over the success of the canal increased daily. As completion seemed apparent, Grant enthusiastically wrote Halleck on March 4 saying that it would be ready in a few days.[85] The next day anticipation increased further with the arrival of a second dredge.

The following night a major setback occurred — the upper dam gave way. Unfortunately the surge of water was insufficient to knock the downstream dam out. Instead, it rushed through the opening in the canal levee flooding the bottom lands south of the railroad embankment. Within a very short time, the crevasse widened to 150 feet, double its original width. Several of the campsites were flooded out. The affected units were evacuated and relocated a few miles upstream at Milliken's Bend. The water level came within 18 inches of topping the canal levee and flooding the camps above the railroad embankment as well.[86]

The engineers made a frantic effort to save the canal. To relieve the pressure on the canal levees, the downstream dam was blasted out. Prime also tried to plug the gap in the canal levee using a coal barge filled with mud, but it

**THE DIPPER DREDGE *SAMPSON* WORKING ON THE ENTRANCE TO THE CANAL.**

*FRANK LESLIE'S, APRIL 4, 1863*

took several days and the aid of a pile driver to finally close the crevasse. Foraging parties were sent out to dismantle service buildings on the various neighboring plantations. They used the planks to strengthen the levee walls of the canal. With the repairs complete the dredges began widening and deepening the canal while troops drilled the stumps, filled them with black powder and blasted them out.[87]

Grant was anxiously awaiting completion of the canal so that he could transport his troops below Vicksburg. On March 12 he wrote Halleck, "The canal is near completion...I will have Vicksburg this month, or fail in the attempt."[88] Prime, in his official report, described the condition of the canal at that time: "...between upper main levee and railroad, mostly dug out to required width, and about six or eight stumps in the canal; between railroad and lower main levee all of the canal to full width with four to six trees and from 12 to 15 stumps in canal."[89] Aside from some minor widening and stump removal, the project was essentially complete except that there was still a breach in the canal levee on the west side below the railroad embankment.

The Confederates were even more convinced than their adversaries that the canal was going to be a success. From across the river they could see the water flowing through the canal. Confederate President Jefferson Davis anxiously telegraphed Lieutenant General John Pemberton, commanding Vicksburg, asking, "What are the operations which indicate that the enemy will get through the canal? Do your guns prove effective against working parties and dredging machines on canal?"[90]

The dipper dredges* operating day and night, gradually worked their way down the canal and by March 15 they had reached the railroad embankment. The Rebels

---

* Dipper dredges in that era were floating steam shovels. The dipper or shovel was mounted on a turntable or rotating platform so that after the shovel was raised, it could rotate to either side in order to drop the dredged material onto an awaiting barge or, if close enough, onto a bank. The depth of dredging was limited by the length of the beam holding the shovel. Based on the contemporary sketch (attached) the shovel capacity was about one cubic yard. These dredges were not self propelled. After being brought to the project by tugs, their forward and lateral movements were achieved by winching cables attached to the shore.

countered by firing at them and by the 17th had the dredges in range, but their accuracy was off. That night they started firing at 10-minute intervals to try to keep the Yankees from sending any boats through the canal.[91]

Two days later the accuracy of the shelling improved to the point that the dredges could no longer work during daylight. That same day Farragut with his flag ship, the *Hartford*, and another of his fleet, the *Albatross*, arrived at Warrenton, about five miles below Vicksburg, after running the batteries on the bluffs at Port Hudson just upriver from Baton Rouge. They began shelling the Confederate batteries opposite the canal but were unsuccessful in preventing them from harassing the dredges.[92]

On March 22, Grant reversed his opinion again and concluded that the canal would be a failure writing, "It is exceedingly doubtful if this canal can be made of any practical use, even if completed. The enemy have established a battery of heavy guns opposite the mouth [exit] of the canal, completely commanding it for one-half its length."[93]

Meanwhile the dredges kept working until the 24th when Rebel gunfire became too hazardous. By Union accounts the Rebels had hurled over 140 shots at the dredges. One of those missiles had gone completely over De Soto Point landing in the river.[94] Ironically, during the day that the dredges departed, the major Confederate gun which had enfiladed the canal exploded.[95] The Union commanders did not realize this until the next day but, rather than take any more chances, the dredges were permanently withdrawn from duty on the canal and a new route was examined. When the dredges were withdrawn they were in the process of widening and deepening the lower half.[96]

Grant, in an effort to meet his promise to Halleck, proposed sending 10 to 12 transports through the canal to ferry troops across the river below Vicksburg under the protection of Farragut's two ships. Either the width of the canal, the Confederate guns or both made him change his mind. Instead, on the morning of March 25, a small contingent, under cover of darkness, marched along the levees below Vicksburg. There they were to await vessels to transport them across the river where they planned to destroy the batteries at Warrenton. Upon advice from Farragut, Porter ordered two rams around De Soto Point to meet the troops and ferry them across the river. In running the batteries the *Lancaster* was sunk and the *Switzerland* was badly disabled, terminating the raid.[97]

Grant had failed to secure a footing above Vicksburg by either Yazoo Pass or Steele's Bayou. His only option was to find a way to get his troops and supplies ferried across the river below Vicksburg. But now the canal, which was soon to bear his name, was also a failure.

Colonel Pride, having replaced Captain Prime as commander of the engineer unit, laid out a route for a new canal about three miles upstream. This project, known as the Duckport Canal, was less ambitious than its predecessor. He would cut a channel one half mile long, 40 feet wide and 7 feet deep from the Mississippi River at Duckport, Louisiana to Walnut Bayou. There, it would connect with Walnut Bayou and exit into the Mississippi at New Carthage, a total of 37 miles by water. Grant intended to use the Duckport Canal to establish a supply route through the waterways. New Carthage would be his ferry landing from which troops could be transported across the Mississippi River to provide a footing on Mississippi soil.[98]

Grant, under much pressure to take Vicksburg, could ill afford another failure from a questionable canal effort. Meanwhile, on March 29 he ordered McClernand's Corps to open a road to march his troops from Milliken's Bend to New Carthage, a point on the river about 20 miles below Vicksburg.[99]

By April 10, 3,500 men were working on the Duckport Canal and Assistant Secretary of War, Charles Dana, sent from Washington to report on progress, estimated the canal to be half complete. By April 13, McClernand had raised the road sufficiently for Pride to blast out the levee separating the Mississippi from the canal. As water rushed into the canal, Pride estimated that he needed about four more days to clear the bayous of trees, stumps and overhanging limbs. With this news, Grant decided that he could wait no longer for this route to be completed, but the work continued because he still needed the waterway to transport coal to the gunboats and transports below Vicksburg and to ship supplies to the army.[100]

**THE RAMS *SWITZERLAND* AND *LANCASTER* RUNNING THE BATTERIES AS SEEN FROM THE LOUISIANA BANK DOWNSTREAM FROM VICKSBURG, DURING THE NIGHT OF MARCH 25, 1863.**

*HARPER'S WEEKLY, APRIL 18, 1863*

**INVESTIGATING WALNUT BAYOU.**

*HARPER'S WEEKLY, MAY 16, 1863*

On April 16, Porter ran the Vicksburg batteries with gunboats and six transports to join the part of Grant's army that had marched by an improvised road through the flooded swamps to New Carthage. On April 18, the transport, *Silver Wave*, steamed up Bayou Vidal to scout the lower end of the 37-mile waterway. Trees and shallow water prevented her from completing the task.[101]

Back at the upper end of the waterway, a tug with barges passed through the canal to Walnut Bayou on April 22 after the canal had been dug deep enough to allow water from the bayou to float them. According to Dana, there was a fifteen-foot depth at the mouth of the canal and six feet of water at the entrance to the bayou where at least four dredges were working. He also noted that the river was falling.[102]

On April 27, Dana reported that "From Milliken's Bend we hear that there is now only six inches of water in Pride's [Duckport] canal at the point where it embouches in the bayou. The dredges are at work but whether they can dig as fast as the river falls is a question. The boats and barges previously got into the bayou will get through, however."[103]

* * *

Once again nature sided with the Confederates and the final canal effort at Vicksburg failed. Nevertheless, Grant succeeded getting below Vicksburg, not by water but by marching his troops overland to New Carthage. From nearby Disharoon's plantation, he ferried his troops across the Mississippi River to Bruinsburg between April 30 and May 1, which led to the siege and ultimate surrender of Vicksburg on July 4, 1863.

The Mississippi River cutoff that Williams started in June of 1862, abandoned in July, and Grant revived in January 1863, ended in failure in March. Nature thwarted both efforts. She punished the troops that worked on the canal worse than if they had been in battle and embarrassed their leaders who had to report their delays and failures to Washington. Grant, frustrated by his loosing battles against the Mississippi River, lamented to Halleck, "The embarrassments

**THREE DIPPER DREDGES WORKING ON THE DUCKPORT CANAL.**

*HARPER'S WEEKLY, MAY 16, 1863*

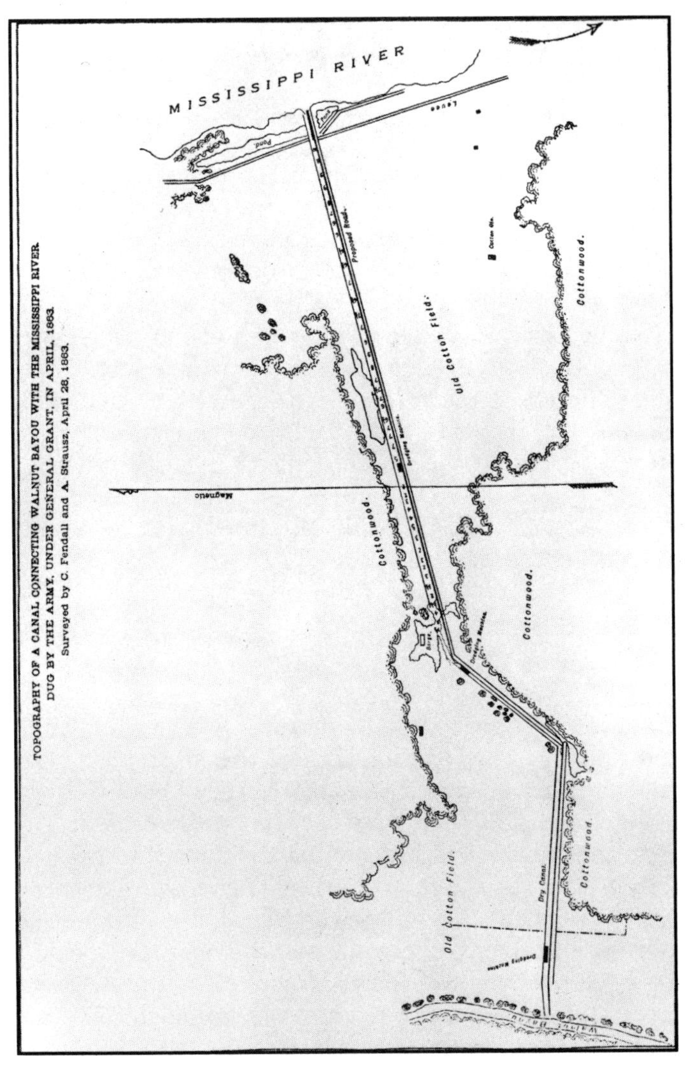

**MAP OF DUCKPORT CANAL.**

*ORN*, 24:596

I have had to contend against on account of extreme high water cannot be appreciated by anyone not present to witness it."[104]

The final irony came in 1876 while Grant was president. As if to mock him, the Mississippi River cut across De Soto Point forming a new channel very near the wartime effort, leaving Vicksburg an inland town.

Nature dramatically proved that the cutoff could have succeeded. Grant, not realizing how close he came to success, rationalized his failure in his memoirs. On that basis, history treats the attempted cutoff as an impractical project. However, if the Union army had procured dredges in January rather than in March, they could have widened and deepened the canal despite the rising river and water table, which so effectively hampered their manual efforts. A timely procurement of the dredges would also have allowed for rerouting the lower end of the canal to either escape the range of artillery located on the bluffs at Warrenton Heights or at least to prevent their being able to enfilade it.

A successful cutoff would have rerouted the Mississippi River away from Vicksburg, eliminating her as a direct threat to Union control of the river.

* * *

After the withdrawal of the dredges, the river gradually receded and by June, the bottom of the attempted cutoff was high and dry.* Over the next thirteen years the river continued to gradually shave away the bank beside the entrance to the failed canal shortening the distance across De Soto Point. During the annual winter flooding in 1876, the Mississippi rose out of its banks as usual, but this time the levees buckled under the pressure of the river and, on April 26, trees fell and dirt was engulfed by the roaring current. The force of the current eroded a new channel about a mile and a half closer to the point of the peninsula than the military effort.

---

* The annual range in river elevation at Vicksburg during the 1860s could be as much as 48 feet.

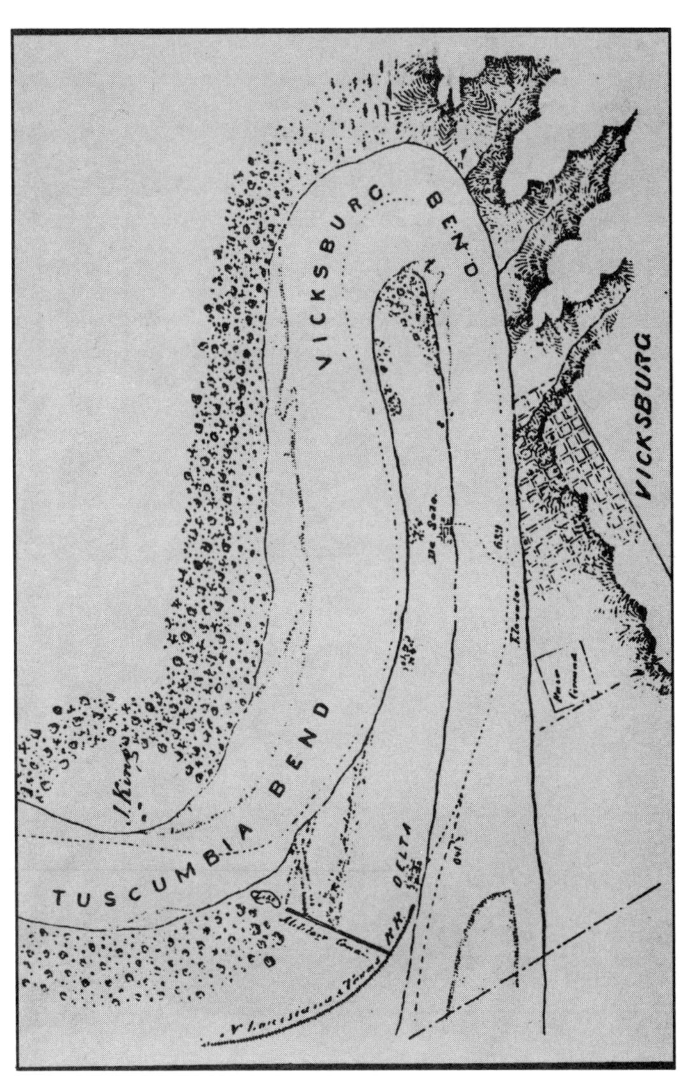


**MAJ. CHARLES R. SUTER'S 1874 MAP SHOWING THE NATURAL NARROWING OF DE SOTO POINT.**

*U.S. ARMY CORPS OF ENGINEERS, MISSISSIPPI RIVER COMMISSION*

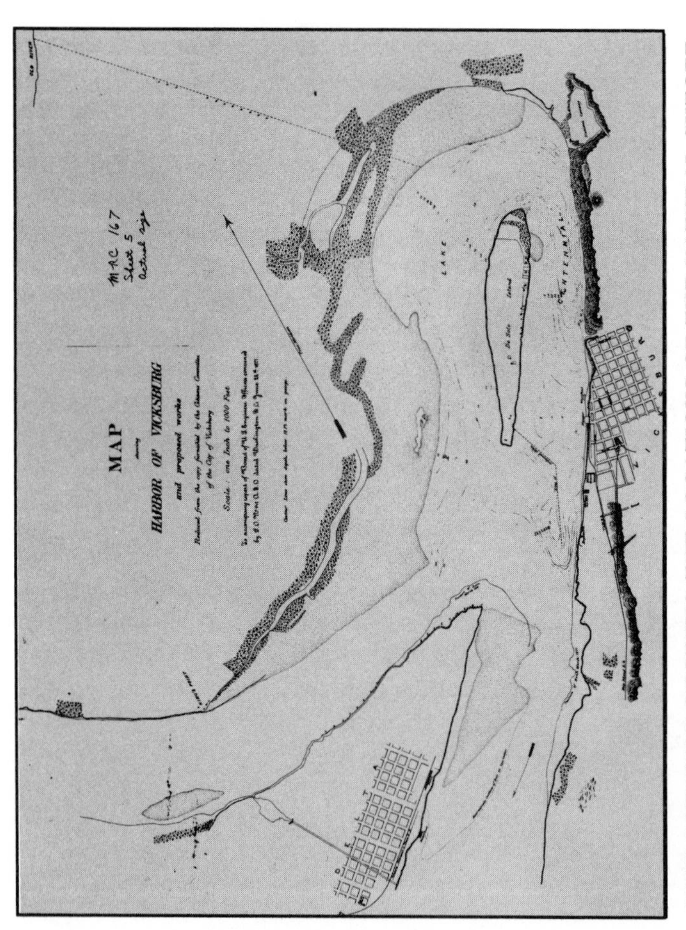


**JUNE 1877 MAP SHOWING THE LOCATIONS OF THE NATURAL CUTOFF, GRANT'S CANAL AND THE HIGH WATER BANKLINE AFTER CUTOFF.**

*U.S. ARMY CORPS OF ENGINEERS, MISSISSIPPI RIVER COMMISSION*

When the floodwaters finally receded, they had sealed off the old river channel. Vicksburg was left stranded. The river had moved about two miles away. Now Vicksburg was an inland town facing onto an ox-bow lake (the former bend in the river) just as Charles Ellet, Jr. had predicted.

Over the next two decades, Vicksburg officials lobbied the Federal government to remedy their misfortune. Finally, the U.S. Army Corps of Engineers diverted the lower end of the Yazoo River into the ox-bow lake at Vicksburg and opened the downstream end of it into the Mississippi River. On January 27, 1903, Vicksburg was once again on the banks of flowing water.

Williams's and Grant's efforts were not without merit. In those days, engineering was more of an art than science. There was no way for the Union army engineers to calculate the size of channel necessary to produce a sufficient velocity across the peninsula in order for the river to erode its own channel. Today, hydraulic analysis shows that if the canal had been completed to the planned dimensions of 60 feet wide and 11 feet deep, that would have produced enough current to erode a permanent channel. Empirically, Ellet knew it would happen and nature vindicated Williams's and Grant's efforts.

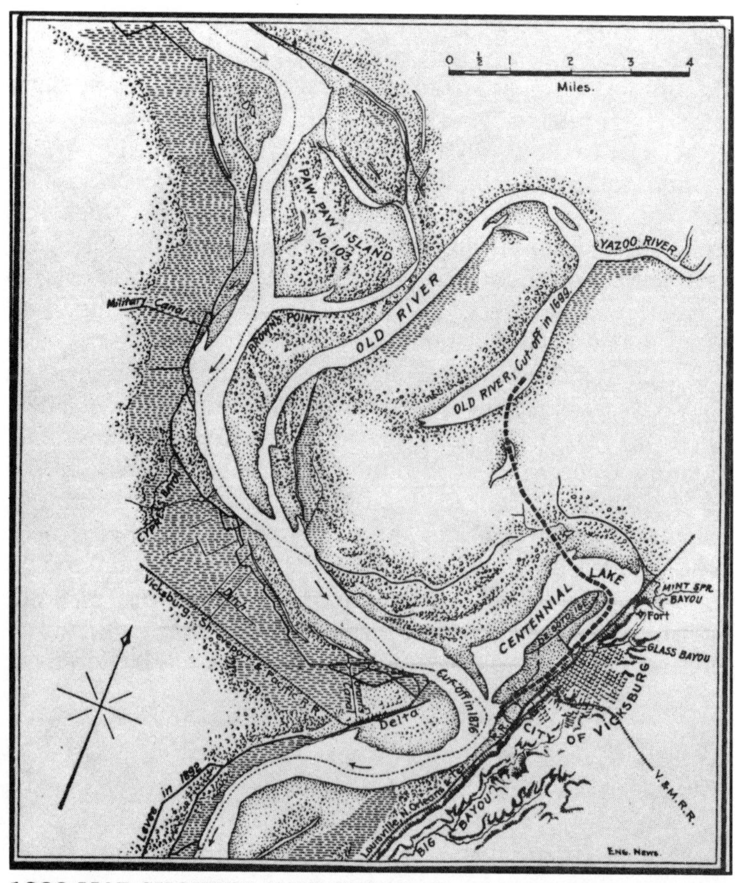


**1883 MAP SHOWING VICKSBURG ON AN OX-BOW LAKE AND THE PROPOSED REROUTING OF THE YAZOO RIVER.**

*ENGINEERING NEWS, MARCH 12, 1903*

# Appendix A

## What Would the Canal Have Accomplished?

The attached map shows the range of Confederate batteries in March of 1863 with respect to the navigable channel of the Mississippi River from Vicksburg south to Grand Gulf. Union vessels could have been and were fired upon from these locations.

By far the most dangerous batteries were at Vicksburg. This was due to the infrastructure which provided the means of transporting larger guns and maintaining a large force. The several mile front of elevated bluffs along the river subjected vessels to more exposure. The other two locations, at and near Grand Gulf, were vulnerable to Union troops had they been able to bypass Vicksburg.

Had the canal been reoriented as Grant requested and completed in early March, troops could have been ferried below Warrenton and discharged onto Mississippi soil without having to cross through swamps or face elevated Confederate batteries on bluffs.

Until Confederate batteries were silenced, supplies could have been protected by floating cotton shields as were employed by the Union in April.

Because canal efforts failed, the Union fleet could not safely pass the several miles of elevated batteries at Vicksburg without considerable risk, and the Union army could not flank Vicksburg until the flood waters receded allowing overland movement south through Louisiana.

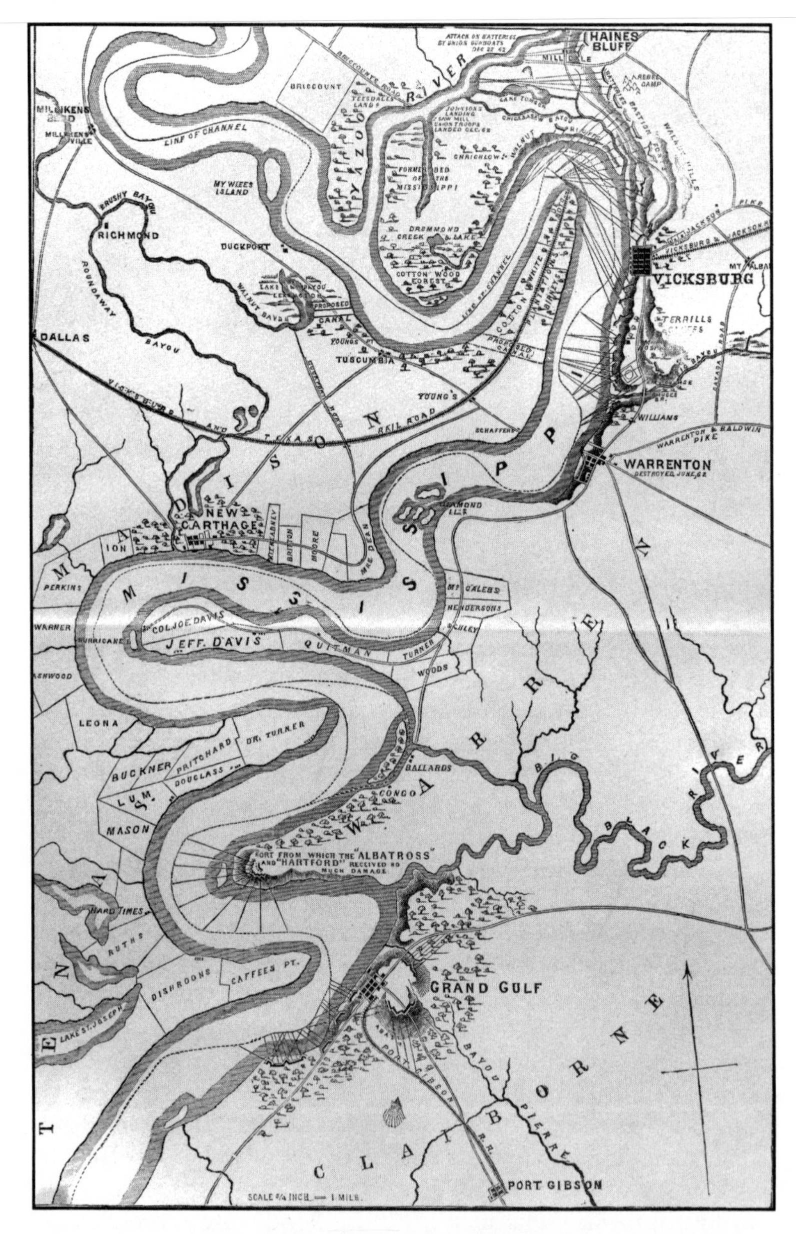


**MAP OF THE MISSISSIPPI RIVER FROM HAINES' BLUFF TO BELOW GRAND GULF.**

*HARPER'S WEEKLY, MAY 23, 1863*

**THE TUG *RUMSEY* ACQUIRED FOR RUNNING THE REBEL BATTERIES AT VICKSBURG.**

*HARPER'S WEEKLY, MAY 30, 1863*

# Appendix B

## Union Army Units Encamped Near or Engaged on the Canal

### May 18 - July 24, 1862

9th Connecticut Infantry Regiment
30th Massachusetts Infantry Regiment
6th Michigan Infantry Regiment
7th Vermont Infantry Regiment
4th Wisconsin Infantry Regiment
2d Battery, Massachusetts Light Artillery
6th Battery, Massachusetts Light Artillery

### January 20 - March 7, 1863

16th Illinois Infantry Regiment
55th Illinois Infantry Regiment
77th Illinois Infantry Regiment
97th Illinois Infantry Regiment
108th Illinois Infantry Regiment
113th Illinois Infantry Regiment
116th Illinois Infantry Regiment
118th Illinois Infantry Regiment
127th Illinois Infantry Regiment
131st Illinois Infantry Regiment
Battery A, 1st Illinois Artillery
Battery B, 1st Illinois Artillery
Battery H, 1st Illinois Artillery
Chicago Merchantile Battery

Thielemann's Battalion Cavalry
16th Indiana Infantry Regiment
49th Indiana Infantry Regiment
54th Indiana Infantry Regiment
60th Indiana Infantry Regiment
67th Indiana Infantry Regiment
69th Indiana Infantry Regiment
77th Indiana Infantry Regiment
83d Indiana Infantry Regiment
4th Iowa Infantry Regiment
11th Iowa Infantry Regiment (except companies C, D, F, & I)
13th Iowa Infantry Regiment
15th Iowa Infantry Regiment
25th Iowa Infantry Regiment
3d Missouri Infantry Regiment
16th Ohio Infantry Regiment
30th Ohio Infantry Regiment
37th Ohio Infantry Regiment
54th Ohio Infantry Regiment
55th Ohio Infantry Regiment
57th Ohio Infantry Regiment
76th Ohio Infantry Regiment
83d Ohio Infantry Regiment
89th Ohio Infantry Regiment
96th Ohio Infantry Regiment
120th Ohio Infantry Regiment
8th Ohio Independent Battery Light Artillery
17th Ohio Independent Battery Light Artillery
17th Wisconsin Infantry Regiment
18th Wisconsin Infantry Regiment
23d Wisconsin Infantry Regiment
4th West Virginia Infantry Regiment

Sources: OR 24:437, 441, 445-47, 450-54; Edwin C. Bearss, *Rebel Victory at Vicksburg* (Little Rock: Pioneer Press, 1963), 290; Bearss, *Iowa Journal of History*, April 1961, "Diary of CPT Bell at Vicksburg; Hosea W. Rood, *Wisconsin at Vicksburg* (Wisconsin-Vicksburg Monument Commission, Madison, Wisconsin, 1914); Henry C. Adams, Jr., *Indiana at Vicksburg* (Indiana-Vicksburg Military Park Commission, Indianapolis, 1911); T. B. Marshall, *History of the Eighty-third Ohio Volunteer Infantry* (Eighty-third Ohio Volunteer Infantry Association, Cincinnati, 1912).

# APPENDIX C

## Sick List of the 7th Regiment Vermont Volunteers, Company H, that were Camped Near Williams's Canal in 1862

The following lists the muster role for one company participating in the Vicksburg campaign under Williams. It shows the effects of the heat, duty and camp conditions on the troops engaged in the canal effort.

| **Date** | | **Number** | | | |
|---|---|---|---|---|---|
| | | **Officers** | | **Enlisted Men** | |
| | | **Duty** | **Sick Call** | **Duty** | **Sick Call** |
| June | 25 | 3 | 0 | 73 | 24 |
| | 26 | 2 | 1 | 64 | 33 |
| | 27 | 2 | 1 | 61 | 36 |
| | 28 | 2 | 1 | 64 | 33 |
| | 29 | 2 | 1 | 65 | 32 |
| | 30 | 2 | 1 | 64 | 33 |
| July | 2 | 2 | 1 | 61 | 36 |
| | 3 | 2 | 1 | 59 | 38 |
| | 4 | 2 | 1 | 47 | 50 |
| | 5 | 2 | 1 | 46 | 51 |
| | 6 | 1 | 2 | 30 | 67 |
| | 7 | 1 | 2 | 51 | 45 |
| | 8 | 1 | 2 | 51 | 45 |

| Date | | Number | | | |
|---|---|---|---|---|---|
| | | Officers | | Enlisted Men | |
| | | Duty | Sick Call | Duty | Sick Call |
| June | 9 | 1 | 2 | 47 | 49 |
| | 10 | 1 | 2 | 48 | 48 |
| | 11 | 2 | 1 | 45 | 51 |
| | 12 | 2 | 1 | 49 | 47 |
| | 13 | 2 | 1 | 53 | 43 |
| | 14 | 2 | 1 | 41 | 55 |
| | 15 | 2 | 1 | 39 | 57 |
| | 16 | 2 | 1 | 39 | 57 |
| | 17 | 2 | 1 | 43 | 53 |
| | 18 | 1 | 2 | 35 | 61 |
| | 19 | 1 | 2 | 46 | 50 |
| | 20 | 1 | 2 | 46 | 50 |
| | 21 | 1 | 2 | 42 | 54 |
| | 22 | 1 | 2 | 40 | 56 |
| | 23 | 1 | 2 | 34 | 62 |
| | 24 | 1 | 2 | 31 | 57 |

By the end of the Vicksburg campaign, the company had lost 9 men and of those remaining, only 37 percent were officially fit for duty.

Source: Anonymous, *History of the Seventh Regiment Vermont Volunteers* (unpublished), Vermont Historical Society.

# Appendix D

## List of Troops from 30th Iowa Infantry that Died from Disease while Encamped near Grant's Canal in 1863

The following is a list of those that died (and their age) due to the harshness of the weather and camp conditions while bivouacked near Grant's Canal during the winter of 1863. This represents only one of the many regiments camped near the canal.

### Company A

Reason Penrod, 40, February 1
Jacob Wisler, 19, February 8
Asa Bishop, 44, February 27
Samuel Ezell, 19, March 3
Wagoner James Snedaker, 30, March 17

### Company B

James T. Bivin, 21, February 6
James Meritt, Jr., 20, February 20
J. W. Wilson, 19, March 27

### Company C

Gideon Hodges, 44, February 12
3d Corporal Thomas S. Canfield, 20, February 21

### Company D

John W. Clark, 26, February 22
William W. Hicks, 19, February 22
John W. Williamson, 26, March 23

### Company E

4th Sergeant Nathan R. Cole, 34, January 31
Harmon G. Connor, 30, February 26
James D. Shover, 18, March 21

### Company F

Musician Daniel Small, 32, February 2
1st Corporal Thomas J. Toner, 24, February 9
3d Corporal John B. Wray, 21, February 20
Robert E. Drake, 23, February 26
Joshua Philips, 21, March 1
John McClasky, 19, March 18

### Company G

James Parker, 43, February 2
Tazwell Carter, 22, February 13
Solomon Stallman, 44, February 17
6th Corporal Nathan Hendricks, 23, February 19
Albert Johnson, 20, February 27
Lewis Summers, 18, March 1
3d Sergeant William Kirkpatrick, 23, March 12
Nathan Kirkpatrick, 18, April 4

### Company H

George A. Holbrook, 22, February 4
Musician John A. Fetter, 18, February 27
5th Sergeant David Gautz, 35, March 14

### Company I

David Hoffman, 28, Februay 7
George W. Pomroy, 22, February 7
Samuel Murphy, 21, February 16
6th Corporal Samuel Barnes, 19, February 26
Thomas J. Wright, 29, March 4

### COMPANY K

Lorenz Escher, Jr., 40, February 12
Thomas Brown, 23, March 4

Source: James A. Fowler & Miles M. Miller, *History of the Thirtieth Iowa Infantry Volunteers* (Mediapolis, Iowa: T. A. Merrill, Printer, 1908), pages 149–82.

# Endnotes

1. David F. Bastian, "Hydraulic Analysis of Grant's Canal," *The Military Engineer*, July–August 1974, p. 228.

2. Ibid., p. 229.

3. Charles Ellet, Jr., *The Mississippi and Ohio Rivers* (Philadelphia: Lippincott, Grambo, & Co., 1853), pp. 191–92. The State of Louisiana had sponsored Racourci Cut-off in 1848 which isolated some plantations and induced downstream flooding. Concerned by the consequences over the likelihood of cutoffs (both manmade and natural) along the Mississippi River, the United States government had contracted with Ellet to examine the river and report on the status and potential for cutoffs.

4. State of Mississippi, Passed at a called session of the Mississippi Legislature, November 1858 (Jackson, E. Barksdale: 1859) p. 223.

5. *Civil War Naval Chronology 1861–1865* (Washington: Department of the Navy, 1971), p. II–47. Even though Farragut succeeded, after a month-long struggle in March 1862 to get all but one of his ships across the bar and into the mouth of the Mississippi River, he had still not challenged the forts below New Orleans by mid April. Meanwhile Major General John Pope and Flag Officer Andrew H. Foote were working their way down the Mississippi River and defeated the Rebel forces at Island No. 10 on April 7. Confederate Secretary of the Navy Mallory was convinced that the serious threat to New Orleans (and thus Vicksburg) would come from Flag Officer Foote in the upper river rather than from Farragut's fleet below.

6. Edwin C. Bearss, *Rebel Victory at Vicksburg* (Little Rock: Pioneer Press, 1963), pp. 50, 136–37.

7. *Official Records of the Union and Confederate Navy in the War of the Rebellion*, 31 vols. (Washington, 1894–1927), ser. 1, 18:491–2 (hereafter cited as *ORN*).

8. *ORN,* 18:520; Farragut's first round trip from New Orleans to Vicksburg and back combined with his return to Vicksburg through the unmarked and shifting channels of the Mississippi River had taken its toll on his ships. He wrote, "you have the account of my cruise up the river; one of greater anxiety I never had. The elements of destruction to the Navy in this river are beyond anything I ever encountered, and if the same destruction continues the whole navy will be destroyed in twelve months. More anchors have been lost and vessels ruined than I have seen in a lifetime, and those vessels which do not run into others are themselves ran into and crushed in such a manner as to render them unseaworthy."

9. Benjamin F. Butler, *Private and Official Correspondence of General Benjamin F. Butler,* vol. 1 (privately issued), pp. 549–50, 561. *ORN,* 24:549; Porter takes credit as being co-author of the cutoff plan with Cpt. Alden. *OR,* part 2, 10:430–431; General G. T. Beauregard, a trained engineer and familiar with the Mississippi River, was concerned about the prospects of a cutoff even before it was conceived by Butler and Farragut. He wrote to Capt. D. B. Harris, Chief Engineer at Vicksburg on April 21, "Another important consideration is that the peninsula opposite Vicksburg should not be susceptible of being canaled from the river above to the river below, for the passage of the enemy's boats, beyond the reach of the guns of the fort."

10. Benjamin F. Butler, *Private and Official Correspondence of General Benjamin F. Butler,* 1:628.

11. *The War of the Rebellion: A Compilation of the Official Records of the Union and Confederate Armies,* 128 vols. (Washington, 1880–1900) ser. 1, 15:494 (hereafter cited as *OR*).

12. *ORN,* 18:585.

13. *ORN,* 18:639.

14. S. H. Lockett, "The Defense of Vicksburg," *Battles and Leaders of the Civil War,* vol. 3 (New York, 1884), p. 483.

15. Loyall Farragut, *The Life of David Glasgow Farragut, First Admiral of the United States Navy, Embodying his Journals and Letters* (New York, 1879), pp. 276–77.

16. *Harper's Weekly,* vol. 6, no. 291, July 26, 1862, p. 471.

17. *ORN,* 18:625.

18. Frank Moore, ed., *The Rebellion Record,* 8 vols. (New York, 1864), vol. 5, Doc. 545–6.

19. Captain Charles Henry Davis, *Life of Charles Henry Davis, Rear Admiral 1807–1877* (Cambridge, 1899), pp. 259–61.

20. Ibid. It was a popularly held misconception that a protective layer of cohesive clay lay over a thick deposit of sand and if this thin lens of clay could be cut away, then the sand could be easily washed away by the current.

21. *ORN*, 18:625.

22. Ibid., p. 675.

23. Ibid., p. 634.

24. *Harper's Weekly*, vol. 6, no. 292, August 2, 1862, p. 482.

25. G. Mott Williams, "Letters of General Thomas Williams," *American Historical Review*, XIV (January, 1909), p. 324; *ORN*, 15:31–32.

26. RG 24, Deck Logs, Log of the Oneida, July 20, 1862, National Archives, Washington, D.C.

27. G. Mott Williams, p. 324.

28. *ORN*, 19:50–51.

29. William C. Holbrook, *A Narrative of the Services of the Officers and Enlisted Men of the Seventh Regiment of Vermont Volunteers (Veterans) from 1862 to 1866* (New York: American Bank Note Co., 1882), pp. 28–29.

30. *ORN*, 19:49; 23:240–41.

31. D. M. Scales to his father, July 31, 1862, Old Court House Museum, Vicksburg, Mississippi. There are no official records of the number of Union deaths during the summer campaign but the number of graves probably included sailors as well as soldiers.

32. Edward Bacon, *Among the Cotton Thieves*, (Detroit: The Free Press Steam Book and Job Printing House, 1867), p. 12.

33. Diary of George R. Yost, September 23, 1862, Naval Historical Center, Department of the Navy, Navy Yard, Washington, D.C.

34. William P. Chambers, "My Journal," ed. Ruth Polk, *Publications of the Mississippi Historical Society* (Jackson, 1925), vol. v, p. 250.

35. *OR*, series 2, 4:421, 512 & 870; In August, the Federal government agreed to ship about 15,000 prisoners of war to Vicksburg. Instead, 3,900 were delivered to Young's Point, about 12 miles upstream, on board 4 transports. They arrived September 10 after a 12-day journey from Cairo, Illinois.

36. *House Document* 11, 38th Congress, 1st Session, "Report of the Superintendent of the Coast Survey," p. 208.

37. *ORN*, 24:711–12; The raft was constructed across the Yazoo River at Snyder's Mill. In Lieutenant Colonel Lovell's January 26, 1863 report to Pemberton in Vicksburg, he described the river barrier. "A boom is now in position, supporting the second raft, and two booms running from it will support the first one, which will greatly add to its strength. More stone should be put in the crib, against which rests the end of the third raft. It will be necessary to blast the rocks to get the stone required...More chains are necessary to secure the lower end of the first raft."

38. *ORN*, 24:181.

39. *ORN*, 24:149; *OR*, 8:625–26, 630; Brigadier General John Pope ordered Bissell to examine the peninsula opposite Island No. 10 to determine whether a canal could be dug to connect the Mississppi to a bayou which emptied into the river below the enemy fortifications. A 500-yard long route was selected through Cypress Swamp.

40. RG 77, Letters Received,Cpt. Jenney to Prime, February 1, 1863, P1258, Chief of Engineers, National Archives, Washington, D.C.

41. G. Mott Williams, p. 324.

42. *ORN*, 24:181.

43. *OR*, part 1, 24:8.

44. John Logan Power Diary, January 23, 1863, Mississippi State Archives.

45. Alex C. Little Collection, letter to his brother, February 18, 1863, Chicago Historical Society.

46. *An Iowa Doctor in Blue, the Letters of Seneca B. Thrall, 1862–1864*, State Historical Society of Iowa, Iowa City, 1960, p. 127.

47. *OR*, part III, 24:9.

48. Alex C. Little Collection, letter to his brother, February 18, 1863, Chicago Historical Society.

49. James P. Boyd Diary, January 23, 1863, Illinois State Library.

50. RG 77, Letters Received, Chief of Engineers, P1258, Jenney to Prime, February 1, 1863, National Archives.

51. *OR*, part III, 24:9.

52. *OR*, part I, 24:10.

53. *OR*, part III, 24:9.

54. *ORN*, 24:204.

55. *OR*, part III, 24:12–3.

56. Ibid., p. 10.

57. *OR*, part I, 24:10.

58. William L. Brown Collection, letter to his father, February 1, 1863, Chicago Historical Society.

59. RG 77, Letters Received, Chief of Engineers, P1258, Prime to Totten, January 29, 1863, National Archives.

60. Ibid.

61. *Vicksburg Whig*, February 14, 1863.

62. Ibid., February 20, 1863.

63. Ibid., January 30, 1863.

64. *OR,* part I, 24:120.

65. Ibid., p. 14.

66. *OR,* part III, 24:32.

67. *OR,* part III, 24:37–38.

68. *ORN,* 24:319–320.

69. *ORN,* 24:242–243.

70. *OR,* part I, 24:119.

71. Ibid., p. 120.

72. Ibid., p. 120–21.

73. *Indiana at Vicksburg* (Indianapolis,W. B. Burford, 1910), p. 355.

74. Charles A. Willison, *With the 76th Ohio Volunteer Infantry in the Civil War* (unpublished manuscript), Vicksburg National Military Park.

75. Jacob B. Ritner Collection, Letter no. 9, Jake to Emeline, February 15, 1863, State Historical Society of Iowa.

76. William L. Brown Collection, letter, W. D. Brown, February 22, 1863, Chicago Historical Society.

77. *OR,* part III, 24:18.

78. RG 107, Records of the Office of the Secretary of War, M-504, reel 184, Prime to Grant, February 16, 1863, National Archives, Washington, D.C.

79. *OR,* part III, 24:18.

80. *Vicksburg Daily Whig,* February 18, 1863.

81. *OR,* part I, 24:120–21.

82. *Frank Leslie's,* February 21, 1863, no. 386, vol. xv, p. 338.

83. *OR,* part I, 24:121.

84. *ORN,* 23:402; ibid., 24:710.

85. Parson Papers, Grant to Col. Lewis B. Parsons, March 3, 1863, Illinois State Historical Library.

86. *OR,* part III, 24:89.

87. *OR,* part I, 24:122–23.

88. Ibid., p. 19.

89. Ibid., p. 122.

90. *ORN,* 24:70.

91. *ORN,* 24:508.

92. Alex R. Miller Collection, *Louisiana State University Archives.*
93. *ORN,* 20:8–9.
94. *ORN,* 24:508.
95. *OR,* part III, 24:145–46.
96. Ibid., p. 147.
97. Ibid., p. 136–37.
98. Ibid., p. 26.
99. *OR,* part I, 24:123.
100. Ibid., pp. 47–48, 73, 79.
101. Ibid., p. 77.
102. Ibid., p. 78.
103. Ibid., p. 81.
104. Ibid., p. 29.

# Bibliography


**Manuscript Sources**

Baylor University Library:
John Amsler Collection

Chicago Historical Society:
William Liston Brown Collection
Alexander C. Little Collection
Dabney Herndon Maury Collection

Collection of V. Crowell, Middleburo, Mass.:
James D. Harris Letters

Historical Society of Delaware:
James Harrison Wilson Diary

Duke University Library:
J. T. Billenstein Journal
Charles B. Tompkins Papers

Emory University Library:
William H. Brotherton Papers

Essex Institute:
John P. Cleaveland Papers

Franklin and Marshall College:
Jonathan M. Foltz Diary

Georgia Department of Archives and History:
Thomas S. Shankle Papers

P. H. Stovall Papers
Boyd-Sitton Family Letters

Illinois State Historical Library:
C. B. Blake Letters
Albert C. Beals Diary
James P. Boyd Diary
W. B. Kennedy Letters
Samuel Willard Collection
John McClernand Papers
Lewis B. Parson Papers
Samuel Gordon Letters
Alexander Shell Letters

Indiana State Library:
Benjamin J. Spooner Collection
Asa E. Sample Diary Letters
George B. Marshall Letters
John Blasdell Letters
George F. Chittenden Papers
Benjamin H. Myers Letters
P. F. Branhamy Letters
Askew Groves Letters
McLaughlin Papers

State Historical Society of Iowa:
Jacob B. Ritner Letters
Perry Phillips Letters
Hiram P. Howe Diary

Louisiana State University Archives:
Rowland Chambers Diary
Moncrief, Robert L. "The Economic Development of the Tallulah Territory," Masters Thesis, Louisiana State University, 1937.
Butler Family Papers
Alex R. Miller Diary

University of Michigan
Bentley Library:
Eli A. Griffin Letters
Engineering-Transportation Library:
Charles Ellet Papers

Mississippi Department of Archives and History:
Charles B. Allen Plantation Book
John Logan Power and Family Papers
Joseph Dill Alison Diary

University of Missouri Library:
John T. Buegal Diary

National Archives:
Record Group 77. Chief of Engineers Letters Received.
Record Group 92. Water transportation file.
Record Group 107. Records of the Office of the Secretary of War.
Record Group 24. Deck logs (for the following U.S. vessels):
*A. Houghton, Adolph Hugel, Arletta, Benton, Black Hawk, Brooklyn, C. P. Williams, Carondelet, Dan Smith, George Mangham, Horace Beals, J. C. Kuhn, John Griffith, Katahdin, Kennebec, Kineo, Miami, Norfolk Packet, Octorara, Oliver H. Lee, Oneida, Orvetta, Owasco, Para, Pinola, Racer, Red Rover, Sciota, Sophronia, T. A. Wood, Tennessee, Tyler, William Bacon, Winona, Wissahickon.*

Southern Historical Collection, University of North Carolina Library:
Mahala P. H. Roach Diary
Charles A. Dimon Papers

Naval Historical Center, Department of the Navy, Navy Yard, Washington, D.C.:
George R. Yost Diary

Old Court House Museum, Vicksburg, Miss.
D. M. Scales Papers

Historical Society of Pennsylvania:
James C. Biddle Papers

Princeton University Library:
Junius Wilson MacMurray Diary

Tennessee State Library and Archives:
Journal of G. R. Elliot Letters

John J. Blair Diary
J. A. Turley Letters

Tulane University Library:
Bartlet-Basore Papers

Vicksburg National Military Park:
F. W. Curtenius Diary
E. T. Eggleston Diary
J. H. Hoit Letters
Alexander Shell Diary
John Ruchman Letters
J. E. Stowbridge Letters
Thomas Taylor Letters
Charles A. Willison. "With the 76th Ohio Volunteer Infantry in the Civil War" (unpublished manuscript)

City Hall, Vicksburg, Mississippi:
Minute Book, March 19, 1860-December 2, 1869

Vermont Historical Society:
Rollin M. Green Letters
Anonymous, "History of the Seventh Regiment, Vermont Volunteers, Record of Company H."

Vigo County Public Library, Terre Haute, Indiana:
John E. Wilkins Diary

State Historical Society of Wisconsin:
Daniel Jewett Letters
Josiah Noonan Collection
Fyfe Family Papers
Robert Steel Collection
Edgar Richmond Papers
Levi Shell Letters

**Newspapers**

Use was made of numerous newspaper files. Newspapers quoted in the text include:

*De Bow's Review*, *Frank Leslie's illustrated*, *Harper's Weekly*, Jackson *Daily Mississippean*, *Natchez Daily Courier*, *New Orleans Daily Picayune*, *New York Tribune*, Shreveport *Southwestern*, *Vicksburg Daily Evening Citizen*, *Vicksburg Daily Herald*, *Vicksburg Daily Times*, *Vicksburg Daily Whig*, *Vicksburg Weekly Whig*.

**Printed Sources**

Anderson, Ephraim McD. *Memoirs: Historical and Personal; Including the Campaigns of the First Missouri Confederate Brigade.* Notes and foreword by Edwin C. Bearss. Dayton, Ohio: Morningside Bookshop, 1972. First published in 1868.

Anderson John Q., ed. *Brokenburn: The Journal of Kate Stone, 1861-1867.* Baton Rouge: Louisiana State University Press, 1955.

Anonymous. *In and About Vicksburg.* Vicksburg: Gilbralter, 1890.

Abrams, Alexander S. *A Full and Detailed History of the Siege of Vicksburg.* Atlanta: Intelligencer Steam Power Press, 1863.

Bacon, Edward. *Among the Cotton Thieves.* Detroit: The Free Press Steam Book and Job Printing House, 1867.

Badeau, Adam. *Military History of U. S. Grant.* New York: D. Appleton & Co., 1881.

Bearss, Edwin C. *Rebel Victory at Vicksburg.* Published by the Vicksburg Centennial Commemoration Commission. Little Rock, Ark.: Pioneer Press, 1963.

Bearss, Edwin C. *Hardluck Ironclad.* Baton Rouge: Louisiana State University Press, 1966.

Bearss, Edwin C. *Decision in Mississippi.* Jackson, Miss: Mississippi Commission on the War Between the States, 1962.

Bearss, Edwin C. *Vicksburg Campaign.* Dayton, Ohio: Morningside Bookstore, 1991.

Black, Robert C. *The Railroads of the Confederacy.* Chapel Hill: University of North Carolina Press, 1952.

Chase, Edward. *The Memorial Life of General William Tecumseh Sherman.* Chicago: R. S. Peale & Co., 1891.

"Chief Engineer's Report." *Vicksburg, Shreveport and Texas Railroad Co.*, September 20, 1856.

*Civil War Naval Chronology*. Compiled by Naval History Division, Navy Department. Washington, D.C.: Government Printing Office, 1971.

Coggins, Jack. *Arms and Equipment of the Civil War.* New York: Doubleday,1962.

Corliss, Carlton J. *Main Line of Mid-America.* New York: Creative Age Press, 1850.

Cramer, Zadok. *The Navigator,* eighth edition. Anne Arbor: University Microfilms.

Davis, Jefferson. *The Rise and Fall of the Confederate Government.* Cranbury, N.J.: Thomas Yoseloff, 1958.

Ellet, Charles, Jr. *The Mississippi and Ohio Rivers.* Philadelphia: Lippincott, Grambo, and Co., 1853.

Evans, Clement A., ed. *Confederate Military History.* Atlanta: Confederate Publishing Co., 1899.

Everhart, William C. *Vicksburg*: Historical Handbook No. 21. Washington, D.C.: Government Printing Office, 1961.

Fiske, John. *The Mississippi Valley in the Civil War.* Boston and New York: Houghton, Mifflin and Company, 1900.

Foltz, C. S. *Surgeon of the Seas.* Indianapolis: Bobbs-Merrill, 1931.

Gift, George W. "The Story of the Arkansas", Southern Historical Society Papers, Vol. XII. Richmond: 1884.

Gosnell, H. Allen, *Guns of Western Waters.* Baton Rouge: Louisiana State University Press, 1949.

Greene, Francis Vinton. *The Mississippi* (Campaigns of the Civil War, vol. 8). New York: Charles Scribner's Sons, 1882.

Guernsey, Alfred H., and Henry M. Alden. *Harper's Pictorial History of the Great Rebellion.* 2 vols. Chicago: McDonnell Bros., 1866, 1868.

Headley, J. T. *Farragut and our Naval Commanders.* New York: E. B. Treat, 1867.

Headley, J. T. *The Life and Travels of General Grant.* Philadelphia: Hubbard Bros., 1879.

Hoehling, A. A. *Vicksburg: 47 Days of Siege.* Englewood Cliffs, N.J.: Prentice-Hall, 1969.

Hoppin, J. M. *Life of Andrew Hull Foote.* New York: Harper, 1874.

Hunter, Louis C. *Steamboats on the Western Rivers.* Cambridge, Mass.: Harvard University Press, 1949.

Johnson, Robert V. and Clarence C. Buel, eds., *Battles and Leaders of the Civil War.* New York: The Century Co., 1884-1888.

Lossing, Benson J., *Pictorial History of the Civil War.* 3 vols. Philadelphia, 1866-1868.

Lowery, Walter McGehee. "Navigational Problems at the Mouth of Mississippi River, 1698-1880." Ph.D. Dissertation Series, Vanderbilt University, 1956.

Lytle, William M. *Merchant Steam Vessels of the United States, 1807-1868.* Mystic, Conn: The Steamship Historical Society of America, 1952.

Mahan, A. T. *Admiral Farragut.* New York: D. Appleton and Company, 1897.

Mahan, D. H. *An Elementary Course of Military Engineering.* New York: John Wiley and Son, 1867.

Merrill, James M. *William Tecumseh Sherman.* Chicago, New York, San Francisco: Rand, McNally & Company, 1971.

Messner, William F. "The Vicksburg Campaign of 1862: A Case Study in the Federal Utilization of Black Labor." *Louisiana History,* vol. 16 (fall 1975), 371-381.

Miers, Earl Schenck. *The Web of Victory: Grant at Vicksburg.* New York: Alfred A. Knopf, 1955.

Milligan, John D. *Gunboats Down the Mississippi.* Annapolis: United States Naval Institute, 1965.

Moore, Frank, ed. *The Rebellion Record, A Diary of American Events.* New York: D. Van Nostrand Publisher, 1867.

Parton, James. *General Butler in New Orleans. History of the Administration of the Department of the Gulf in the Year 1962.* New York: Mason Brothers, 1864.

Pemberton, John C. *Pemberton: Defender of Vicksburg.* Chapel Hill, N.C.: The University of North Carolina Press, 1942.

Porter, David Dixon. *The Naval History of the Civil War.* New York: The Sherman Publishing Company, 1886.

Richardson, Albert D. *A Personal History of Ulysses S. Grant.* Hartford: American Publishing Company, 1868.

"Report of the President and Director of the Vicksburg, Shreveport and Texas Railroad Co. to the Legislature of Louisiana." Baton Rouge: Daily Advocate, 1857.

"Report of the State Engineers." *Louisana Senate Journal, 1849.*

"Report of the Superintendent of the Coast Survey." *House Document 11, 38th Congress, 1st Session.*

Robins, Edward. *William T. Sherman.* Philadelphia: George W. Jacobs & Company, 1905.

Roman, Alfred. *Military Operations of General Beauregard In the War Between the States, 1861 to 1865.* New York: Harper and Brothers, 1884.

Scharf, J. Thomas. *History of the Confederate States Navy.* Atlanta: W. H. Shepard, 1887.

Soley, J. R. *Admiral Porter.* (Great Commander Series. Edited by James Grant Wilson.) New York: D. Appleton & Company, 1903.

Steiner, Paul E. *Disease in the Civil War, Natural Biological Warfare in 1861-1865.* Springfield: Charles C. Thomas, 1968.

Vilas, William Freeman. *A View of the Vicksburg Campaign.* Wisconsin History Commission, 1908.

Walker, Peter F. *Vicksburg: A People at War, 1860-1865.* Chapel Hill, N.C.: The University of North Carolina Press, 1960.

West, Richard S. *The Second Admiral, A Life of David Dixon Porter, 1813-1891.* New York, 1937.

Winters, John D. *The Civil War in Louisiana.* Baton Rouge: Louisiana State University Press, 1963.

Wheeler, Richard. *The Siege of Vicksburg.* New York: Thomas Y. Crowell Co., 1978.

**Regimental Histories, Memoirs, Personal Reminiscences, Diaries and Correspondence**

Bearss, Edwin C. "Diary of CPT Bell at Vicksburg." *Iowa Journal of History.* State Historical Society, Iowa City, April 1961.

Bell, Irvin Wiley. *This Infernal War, The Confederate Letters of Sgt. Edwin H. Fay.* Austin, Tex: University of Texas Press, 1958.

Benedict, G. G. *Vermont in the Civil War, A History of the Part Taken by the Vermont Soldiers and Sailors in the War for the Union, 1861-5.* Burlington, Vt.: The Free Press Association, 1888.

Bettersworth, John K. and James W. Silver, ed. *Mississippi in the Confederacy As They Saw It.* Baton Rouge: Louisiana State University Press, 1961.

Butler, Benjamin F. *Private and Official Correspondence of General Benjamin F. Butler.* Norwood, Mass: Privately issued, 1917.

Butler, Benjamin F. *Autobiography and Personal Reminiscences of Major General Benjamin F. Butler: Butler's Book.* Boston: A. M. Thayer, 1892.

Chambers, William P. "My Journal." Edited by Ruth Polk. *Publications of the Mississippi Historical Society, vol V.* Jackson, Miss.: 1925.

Dana, Charles A. *Recollections of the Civil War.* New York: D. Appleton and Company, 1898.

Davis, Charles H. *Life of Charles Henry Davis, Rear Admiral, 1807-1877.* New York: Houghton Mifflin, 1899.

Farragut, Loyall. *The Life of David Glasgow Farragut, First Admiral of the United States Navy. Embodying his Journal and Letters.* New York: D. Appleton and Company, 1879.

Fowler, James A. and Miles M. Miller. *History of the Thirtieth Iowa Infantry Volunteers.* Mediapolis, Iowa: T. A. Merrill, 1908.

Fowler, Smith W. *Autobiographical Sketch of Capt. S. W. Fowler, Late of the 6th Michigan Infantry*. Manistee, Mich.: 1878.

Fox, Gustavus Vasa. *Confidential Correspondence of Gustavus Vasa Fox, Assistant Secretary of the Navy, 1861-1865.* Edited by Robert M. Thompson and Rich Wainwright. New York: Naval Historical Society, 1917.

Gift, George W. "The Story of the Arkansas," *Southern Historical Society Papers*. Vol. XII, Richmond: 1884.

Goldsborough, W. W. *The Maryland Line in the Confederate Army, 1861-1865*. Port Washington, New York: Kennikat Press, 1972.

Grant, Ulysses S. *Personal Memoirs*. New York: Charles L. Webster, 1894.

Hall, Winchester. *The Story of the 26th Louisiana Infantry, in the Service of the Confederate States.* [No publisher or place], 1888.

Hicken, Victor. *Illinois In The Civil War.* Urbana: University of Illinois Press, 1966.

Hoffman, Wickham. *Camp, Court and Seige.* New York: Harper, 1877.

Holbrook, William C. *A Narrative of the Services of the Officers and Enlisted Men of the 7th Regiment of Vermont Volunteers from 1862 to 1866.* New York: American Bank Note Company, 1882.

Howe, Henry W. *Passages from the Life of Henry Warren, Consisting of Diary and Letters Written During the Civil War, 1861-1865, a Condensed History of the Thirtieth Massachusetts.* Lowell, Mass.: Courier-Citizen, 1899.

*Indiana at Vicksburg.* Compiled by Henry C. Adams. Indianapolis: W. B. Burford, 1910.

Jackson, Joseph Orville, ed. *Some of the Boys, the Civil War Letters of Isaac Jackson, 1862-1865.* Carbondale: Southern Illinois University Press, 1960.

Jenney, William L. B. "Personal Recollections of Vicksburg." *Military Essays and Recollections.* Chicago: Thomas Barbour, 1899.

Kirwan, A. D., ed. *Johnny Green of the Orphan Brigade: The Journal of a Confederate Soldier.* Lexington: University of Kentucky Press, 1956.

Marshall, T. B. *History of the Eighty-third Ohio Volunteer Infantry.* Cincinnati: 1912.

Murray, Thomas Hamilton. *History of the Ninth Regiment, Connecticut Volunteer Infantry, "The Irish Regiment," in the War of the Rebellion, 1861-65.* New Haven: The Price, Lee & Adkins Co., 1903.

*Official Records of the Union and Confederate Navies in the War of the Rebellion.* Washington: GPO, 1894-1922.

*Official Roster of the Soldiers of the State of Ohio in the War of the Rebellion, 1861-1866.* Cleveland: WPA, 1938.

Osborn, B. S., ed. *The Cruise of the U. S. Flag-Ship Hartford, 1862-1863...From the Private Journal of William C. Holton.* New York: L. W. Paine, Printer, 1863.

Pitzman, Julius. "Vicksburg Campaign Reminiscences." *The Military Engineer,* vol. 15, no. 80 (March/April 1923): 112-15.

*Revised Roster of Vermont Volunteers.* Compiled by Theodore S. Peck. Montpelier, Vt.: Watchman Publishing Co., 1892.

Porter, David D. *Incidents and Anecdotes of the Civil War.* New York: D. Appleton and Company, 1886.

Read, Charles W. "Reminiscences of the Confederate States Navy," *Southern Historical Society Papers,* vol. 1. Richmond: 1876.

*The Secret Diary of Robert Patrick, 1861-1865.* Edited by F. Jay Taylor. Baton Rouge: Louisiana State University Press.

Selfridge, Thomas O. *Memoirs of Thomas O. Selfridge, Jr., Rear Admiral, U.S.N.* New York: G. P. Putnam's Sons, 1924.

Sherman, William T. *Memoirs.* 2 vols. New York: D. Appleton and Company, 1875.

Simon, John Y., ed. *The Papers of Ulysses S. Grant,* vol. 7: *December 9, 1862-March 31, 1863.* Carbondale, Ill.: Southern Illinois University Press, 1979.

Soule, Harrison. "From the Gulf to Vicksburg, by Harrison Soule, Major 6th Michigan Infantry." *Military Order of the Loyal Legion-Michigan,* Vol. II., 1894.

Temple, Wayne C. *Civil War Letters of Henry C. Bear.* Harrogate, Tenn.: Lincoln Memorial University Press, 1961.

*Tennesseans in the Civil War, A Military History of Confederate and Union Units with Rosters of Personnel.* Nashville: 1964.

Thorndike, Rachel Sherman, ed. *The Sherman Letters, Correspondence Between General and Senator Sherman from 1837 to 1891.* New York: AMS Press, 1894.

Todd, William (of Co. B). *The 79th Highlanders, New York Volunteers in the War of the Rebellion, 1861-1865.* Albany: Press of Brandon, Barton & Co., 1886.

*The War of the Rebellion: A Compilation of the Official Records of the Union and Confederate Armies.* Washington: GPO, 1880-1902.

Throne, Mildred, ed. *The Civil War Diary of Cyrus F. Boyd, Fifteenth Iowa, 1861-1863.* Iowa City: State Historical Society of Iowa, 1953.

Throne, Mildred, ed. "An Iowa Doctor in Blue, The Letters of Seneca B. Thrall, 1862-1864." *Iowa Journal of History.* Iowa City: April 1960.

Tunnard, W. H. *A Southern Record: the History of the Third Regiment, Louisiana Infantry.* Preface, notes, and roster by Edwin C. Bearss. Dayton, Ohio: Morningside Bookshop, 1970. First published in 1866.

Walke, Henry. *Naval Scenes and Reminiscences.* New York: F. R. Reed, 1877.

Welles, Gideon. *The Diary of Gideon Welles* (With a preface by Edgar T. Welles and an introduction by John T. Morse, Jr.). Boston: Houghton Mifflin, 1911.

Williams, G. Mott. "Letters of General Thomas Williams." *American Historical Review,* XIV, 1909. pp. 304-328.

*Wisconsin at Vicksburg, report of the Wisconsin-Vicksburg Monument Commission.* Compiled by Hosia W. Rood. Madison: 1914.

Whitcomb, Caroline E. *History of the Second Massachusetts Battery (Nims' Battery) of Light Artillery, 1861-1865, Compiled from Records of the Rebellion, Official Reports, Diaries and Roster.* Concord: Rumford Press, 1912.

Yeary, Mamie. *Reminiscences of the Boys in Gray, 1861-1865.* Dallas: Smith and Lamar, 1912.

# INDEX